ON THE WAY

ON THE WAY

Learning and Living as a Christian

RICHARD BEWES

KINGSWAY PUBLICATIONS
EASTBOURNE

ISBN 0 86065 294 7

NIV = New International Version
     © New York International Bible Society 1978

RSV = Revised Standard Version
     copyrighted 1946, 1952, © 1971, 1973 by the
     Division of Christian Education of the National
     Council of the Churches of Christ in the USA

Front cover photo: Tony Stone Photolibrary—London

Printed in Great Britain for
KINGSWAY PUBLICATIONS LTD
Lottbridge Drove, Eastbourne, E. Sussex BN23 6NT by
Cox & Wyman Ltd, Reading.
Typeset by Nuprint Services Ltd, Harpenden, Herts.

*This book is dedicated to
the family—to Liz, my dearest partner, and to
Timothy, Wendy and Stephen—who all put up with my
writing activities with stoic endurance
and loving support.*

Contents

Foreword

I'm glad to commend this little book for two big reasons. Firstly, because Richard Bewes is one of those balanced Christian teachers I respect immensely. I'll spare his blushes, but suffice it to say that Richard's ministry has relevance, honesty and authority, and I for one am only too grateful for the chance to learn from him.

Secondly, any time you give to this book will be time well spent. Very simply, it will do you good. There is no imposition of cranky whims or extreme opinions—only signposts towards the totally reliable and all-time truths—the ones I have been slowly uncovering over these last nineteen years, and which for me have opened a whole new dimension of living.

Don't get it wrong. Progressing as a Christian—which is what this book is about—is a million miles away from arid religious theory. In show-business I am bombarded with all sorts of weird and wonderful spiritual speculation and, for the most part, it leads to a frustrating dead end. Christian truth, on the other hand, concerns my life today—whether I'm walking the dogs, singing on stage, recording in studios, or playing tennis!

And something else that's important—Richard doesn't do your thinking for you. There are no pat answers served up for easy consumption. Assuming that you approach with an inquisitive and honest mind, I have a shrewd suspicion that your understanding of life as a Christian will tally with that of Bible-believing Christians the world over.

I once recorded a song called 'The Joy Of Living'. The lyrics didn't explain how to achieve it. This book does!

CLIFF RICHARD
February 1984

Introduction

Years ago as a young lad in Nairobi, Kenya, I asked my Uncle Anstis to write something in my schoolboy autograph album.

'Something serious, or funny?' he enquired, pen poised.

I was already primed with my answer. My brother Peter had just obtained a funny autograph, and I was under strict instructions not to devalue his own autograph by asking for another funny.

'Serious please, Uncle Anstis', I meekly answered. Within a couple of minutes the little poem stared up at me from my album:

> *I am only one, but I am one!*
> *I cannot do everything, but I can do something;*
> *What I can do, I ought to do,*
> *And what I ought to do*
> *By the grace of God I will do.*

The words have always been a help to me. They remind me of the uniqueness—and powerful potential—of the individual. We need these reminders today. We live in a society that is dazzled by swarming statistics, dwarfed by towering power structures.

This little book is designed to help those who are new to the Christian life, who are anxious to establish their own precious identity in the family of God. As you begin to read these pages, you may not know a thing about discipleship; perhaps you have only just made a beginning with God. I have written this to try and give you some guidelines, some encouragement, and a degree of spiritual lift-off! The book can also be used on a group level—perhaps for a confirmation or discipleship class. It is not anchored to any one Christian church or denomination. I have simply tried to be biblical. After every two chapters there is an opportunity for group study, with questions set down to stimulate discussion.

In my Bible quotations, I have not confined myself to any one version—I have felt free to roam between the different translations.

May God bless you as you turn these pages; and may he encourage us to live for him in this exciting but confused century in which we have been placed.

RICHARD BEWES
All Souls Church, Langham Place

PART ONE

The Decision-Makers

A Christian is, in essence, somebody personally related to Jesus Christ. Christianity without Christ is a chest without a treasure, a frame without a portrait, a corpse without breath. Christ comes to each of us with an individual summons: 'Come to me', 'follow me'. And the Christian life begins as, however hesitantly and falteringly, we respond to his call.

Then as we start following him, we discover to our increasing and delighted surprise, that a personal relationship to Christ is a many-sided, many-coloured, many-splendoured thing. We find that he is our mediator and our foundation, our life-giver and our lord, the secret and goal of our living, our lover and our model.

John Stott, Focus on Christ,
Collins

Christianity, if false, is of no importance, and if true, of infinite importance. The one thing it cannot be is moderately important.

—C. S. LEWIS

I

Play Back the Video

In a London subway one August a jewel thief was
cornered and arrested. The police removed him from
Farringdon underground station and picked up what
they thought was the bag of missing gems. In fact it
was a similar bag belonging to a train driver, George
Nelson.

When the train driver reached the end of the line he
felt a little peckish and opened his lunch bag, only to
recoil with amazement at the sight of thousands of
pounds worth of jewellery. Miles away the police
opened up their bag and were equally dumbfounded
to be confronted by a flask of tea and three cheese
sandwiches.

Which goes to show that you can never be too sure
of your facts. Appearances can deceive!

This book is about living and growing as a Christian—but first we must make sure we've picked up the
genuine article! Let's step back in time and retrace the
steps that led us to our present faith in Christ. Perhaps
we were among those deceived by the externals of
Christianity and the Church...those forbidding
buildings...the antiquity...the bat-ridden grave-

yards. And just what lay inside the black covers of that venerable survivor of the centuries, the Bible? Was there anything there for the micro-chip generation— beyond a dust-laden collection of yawning irrelevancies? 'Leave it to the fossil-hunters and professors,' we may have murmured. 'Christianity's a museum piece now.'

Then one day something happened to change our thinking. It could have been any one of a thousand factors. What was it? A book you picked up? A meeting you went to? A personal sorrow? The friendship of a believing Christian? An invitation service at a local church?

What was it? You see, every story is different! I can think of an agnostic whose love of music made him sit up and question himself: *Am I just the product of chance? Does this music simply derive from unthinking matter in the last analysis?* These questions provided the stimulus that brought him finally to Christian belief.

Circumstances and emotions vary considerably every time a person sets out as a disciple of Christ. But the basic reaction is one of discovery and gladness. I remember talking with a Moslem who had turned to Jesus Christ:

'I hear you were recently baptized,' I enthused.

'Yes,' came the grinning reply. 'It was very nice. I liked it!'

I liked it. But why? What is it about Christianity that makes it the jewel haul of a lifetime? What was your own experience? Think about it, and analyse it. Was it the thought of the new friends you would make? I doubt it—though friends there will be. Was it the prospect of the lifting of some of your problems and burdens? Perhaps that was in your mind—but aren't you now already facing a bunch of problems as a result of your belief in Christ? There must be a better reason for being a Christian.

There is, of course. A new Christian expressed it well when she spoke to me at our church prayer gathering. *'In Christianity at last I have found the truth,'* she smiled.

How right! It is an amazing liberation just to have found the truth—for the truth's sake. To know at last who and what I am, what existence is all about, who originated the universe; the significance of my little candle-flame of a life; the possibility of friendship with God...of being forgiven by him...and loved.

What finally unlocked the puzzle? There are millions of us around the world who can answer that question in two words: *Jesus Christ.* When we have been introduced to the Man of Galilee, there is nowhere else to look; he stands alone. Here is God himself in human form, visiting our world, living among us, dying for us—and raising us to the new life with himself, in a living permanent relationship.

Knowing God in the person of Jesus—this is the essence of real Christianity. Karl Barth, who was a great theologian, put it well: 'If one goes wrong here, one is wrong all along the line. If one is at least on the right track here, the whole thing cannot be completely wrong.'

So come back to yourself...to your very own story. Play back the video and make sure that you picked up the correct bag—check that the beginning was *right*! It's worth it. We've only to be off course by a few degrees at the start, for us to be landed in a whole load of bother in a few years' time when the angle of error has widened.

What is the best way of checking? We'll look at the Bible—at the first sermons preached by the early Christians. They had no video, but several of those sermons were recorded, at least in edited form, by Luke, the author of the New Testament book of Acts. How did these early Christians portray this Christianity? What is 'salvation'? Let's follow carefully what the Bible says and do a little checking up...

The basis of salvation—two events

Two things happened, which launched Christianity into being. First, *the death of Jesus*. Christianity's first sermon tells us that there was more to the crucifixion than the tragic killing of an innocent man. Listen to the apostle Peter in full cry:

> This man was handed over to you by God's set purpose and foreknowledge; and you, with the help of wicked men, put him to death by nailing him to the cross (Acts 2:23 NIV).

So God's forgiving purposes for mankind were behind the crucifixion. There, in the person of his Son, God was himself accepting responsibility for the guilt of us all; himself enduring the solitude and banishment that we deserved. As Peter wrote later on in his New Testament letter, 'For Christ died for sins once for all, the righteous for the unrighteous, to bring you to God' (1 Pet 3:18 NIV). The cross meets our greatest need— our guilt!

It is a breathtaking concept: Christ has done everything necessary to remove the barrier of guilt that would otherwise bar me from friendship with God, both in this life and the life to come!

And the other event? Do I need to spell it out? It was *the resurrection of Jesus*. Listen to Peter again in that first great sermon:

> But God raised him from the dead, freeing him from the agony of death, because it was impossible for death to keep its hold on him (Acts 2:24 NIV).

These themes dominate the early chapters of Acts! If the cross was the means by which God had dealt with the guilt of sin, then the resurrection was the evidence and proof that Christ's sacrifice was accepted fully and recognized by God the Father. From then on the world could never be the same again. A man had beaten death decisively! And whoever believes in him shares his resurrection victory (Jn 11:25).

Two events…but everything rests on them. What is our response?

The call of salvation—two responses

Do you remember making a response to the claims of Christ upon your life? Not everybody can point to an exact time or place; and that need not matter—any more than a friend of mine didn't know how old he was! A Ugandan preacher, Festo Kivengere by name, I once asked him,

'How old are you, Festo?'

'I don't know my birthday,' he replied. 'All I know is that my life started some time during the great rinderpest cattle plague in West Uganda!'

When it comes to *spiritual* birth, then, the important question is 'Have we made a response?' Once again the sermons of Acts help us here, for there are two sides to this. First, there is *the response of repentance*. Repentance is a change of mind, leading to a change of direction. It occurs when someone says: 'I have been wrong; but I am willing to admit this, to turn around and seek forgiveness for having crowded God out of my life.' That's the first part of our response—the negative part. And the positive? It is *the response of faith*, which is made as we accept all that Christ has done on our behalf and as we receive him as Lord and Saviour of our lives.

Repentance and faith. They go together. The apostle Peter combines them beautifully in another of his early sermons:

> Repent then, and turn to God, so that your sins may be wiped out (Acts 3:19 NIV).

Let's move on to a third aspect of salvation.

The promise of salvation—two gifts

Yes, it's all a gift. If you think that salvation . . . coming to know Christ . . . being forgiven, is a matter of pulling up your socks, making a new effort, trying a little harder, then you're still holding the wrong bag! We can never *earn* forgiveness and a place in heaven. Christ *died* to achieve for us what we could not do for ourselves—let's not insult him by thinking that we can contribute to our standing with God. It's all free, and we can only accept it (Eph 2:8, 9).

Basically there are two gifts: first, *the gift of forgiveness*, which places us in an altogether new relationship with God. Sinners we shall continue to be for the rest of our lives—but forgiven sinners! We need not wait until we die to find out if God will let us into heaven. We can know, the moment we cease to be a rebel. Such is God's generosity.

But something else is promised through the good news. It is *the gift of the Holy Spirit*. For God does not leave us merely forgiven—yet helpless, like a mewing cat stranded upon a piece of driftwood in the middle of a pond. Part of the offer of salvation is the promised presence of God himself within our lives and personalities, to empower us and motivate us for the life of a Christian.

When people have newly become disciples of Jesus Christ, they will sometimes say, 'I have received *Christ* into my life.' Perhaps you have said this yourself. You were perfectly right—it was indeed Christ that you received; but *technically* it was the *Spirit* of Christ whom you received. Jesus had forewarned his disciples before his bodily departure that he would send 'The Counsellor', the Holy Spirit to indwell them. In this way the promised presence of Jesus himself is with every believer in every country and upon every continent— something that could never have happened when his ministry was confined to Palestine. It is the Spirit who makes us conscious of our new Master, Christ, and reminds us that we belong to him.

Two gifts without price! The wiping of the slate clean, and the power for a new way of life. This is how Peter described God's gifts when calling upon his listeners to respond to the good news...

...so that your sins may be forgiven. And you will receive the gift of the Holy Spirit. The promise is for you and your children and for all who are far off—for all whom the Lord our God will call (Acts 2:38, 39 NIV).

Is this your story? Perhaps it came about in a muddled way, and without you knowing any of the biblical terms... but can you recognize these patterns in your own experience? Use this chapter carefully to check on your own beginnings with Christ. For some of us this may necessitate *a re-affirmation*; a kind of writing over in ink of what has so far only been written in pencil!

You see, no one person's experience is exactly the same as another's. And yet... it *is* the same experience; it is Christ who joins us believers as brothers and sisters of one another, even if we come from different social backgrounds and from different church traditions. *Christ has come into our lives*. The nightmare of aimlessness, uncertainty and guilt is swept into oblivion.

Let me give an illustration to close the chapter. Every so often I have a nightmare. It's this—I find myself back at my college, about to take my final exams all over again! I find myself caught out, unready. Even in my dream I know that something is wrong: 'I shouldn't be here—I'm a London clergyman... perhaps I'll wake up in a moment.' But I don't seem to wake, and the moment of reckoning draws ever near.

And then I do wake up! I can only say that the sense of relief is indescribable. I lie there in the darkness, hugging the truth to myself; *it's all right*. It all happened, way back; I passed!

But come to another nightmare—your own. There *you* are, a miserable, unprepared individual, caught out. You sit down in the examination hall and pick up the question paper and—disaster! Not one question can you even attempt. At that point there's a tap on your shoulder. An insignificant-looking official murmurs in your ear, 'Excuse me, you shouldn't be here.'

'Shouldn't be here?'

'No. You don't have to take this exam. You've already passed.'

'Passed?' The room sways around you.

'That's right. Our records indicate that you don't need to take this exam. Look!' and a scroll of paper is whipped in front of your eyes.

'Your degree,' exclaims the patient official. 'We don't want you here. You can go.'

And slowly you stumble out in a daze into the brilliant sunshine, clutching the degree you never deserved. Gradually the truth sinks in. You've passed!

But this is only a pale reflection of the good news. Jesus expressed it as follows:

> I solemnly assure you that the man who hears what I have to say and believes in the one who has sent me has eternal life. He does not have to face judgment; he has already passed from death into life (Jn 5:24 J. B. Phillips).

The good news then, what is it? It is an announcement *here and now* to the believer of the verdict of our future judgement! We are declared, in Christ, as having *already* passed from death to life, as *already* forgiven and destined for the celestial city of God, *already* indwelt by the Spirit of Christ who seals us for eternity. We know this *now*. The nightmare is over.

Or, to change the metaphor, it is like moving from the old chapter of our lives into the new.

*   *   *   *

To learn: At the end of every chapter try to learn one Bible sentence off by heart—permanently! Learn the sentence with its correct reference (both before and after) so that you can find it easily in your Bible. Like this!

John 3:16 For God so loved the world that he gave his only Son, that whoever believes in him should not perish but have eternal life John 3:16.

Christianity isn't a narcotic that dulls you into obedience. It involves battle—it's excruciating to give up control. But that is why we must not despair if we are struggling. To struggle does not mean we are incorrigible. It means we are ALIVE!

—REBECCA MANLEY PIPPERT

2

The Morning After

'And now for a Tom and Jerry colour cartoon!'

A cheer went up from a hundred and fifty boys and girls crammed into a church hall one December evening. It was an international Christmas party, and the room was brimming with enthusiasm. The lights went down and the projector was switched on for the anticipated movie.

Anticlimax...something was wrong! I froze in my seat. My clerical colleague responsible for hiring the film had been sent the wrong one. Groan! We were watching not Tom and Jerry in colour, but a black and white documentary of the British seaweed industry!

We've all known this experience. The big football match that turns out to be a damp squib...the holiday that got rained off...the overblown political promises at election time followed by the let-down—disillusionment seems to be a built-in part of our living.

Is it part of the Christian package, too? The new believer might understandably think that it was, after even a short time of discipleship. Becoming a follower of Jesus Christ is a little like getting married. There is the period of romance, then the thinking-through stage, followed by the moment of commitment and decision. Then the honeymoon discoveries of a new life...and then it's Monday morning.

Back to the old familiar world! The anxieties of everyday life are upon you again. Yesterday's preacher seems a million miles away in a technicolour world of his own—against which your own monochrome existence seems decidedly...well, anticlimactic. Somehow it's slipped out that you've got in with the church lot, and an invisible barrier seems to have risen between you and your friends. Perhaps even your family relationships are affected.

Do you feel something like this? *I'm in no-man's-land. I don't seem to belong anywhere. It's uncomfortable being a Christian. Yes, I made a decision to accept Christ, but it's landed me with a whole bundle of problems. If only my friends understood. If only I could really live like a Christian now. If only I wasn't such a horrible person. If only I hadn't sworn like that a moment ago. Maybe I was taken for a ride. Maybe I'm not a Christian at all. Perhaps I have to go back to square one and start all over again.*

No, don't despair! A person who has just responded to the call of Jesus Christ has made the biggest, the most far-reaching decision of a lifetime. It's upsetting enough to change jobs...to move house. When our whole way of looking at life goes through a transformation and finds a new centre in God, we get rocked to our very foundations. Doubts and misgivings will swirl around us—they are an important part of the growing process.

So how do I know that I'm a Christian? Let's look at signposts we can be sure of right away. I call them the three W's:

The word of God

After all it was God's revealed truth—the Bible—that started this whole business off! It was in response to its message that we received Christ at all.

Very well then, it is to the Bible that I must turn as a new believer, if I am to find any firm assurance that God actually *did* something in me and for me when I turned in faith to his Son Jesus. It's no use trusting in how I now *feel*; my emotions will play me false time and again. They will fluctuate with the weather, the fortunes of my favourite football team or the latest developments on the Stock Exchange!

The newest, rawest Christian recruit can cling like a limpet to God's promises from the word go. What promises are we talking about? The New Testament is brimming with them...

> Yet to all who received him, to those who believed in his name, he gave the right to become children of God (Jn 1:12 NIV).

> Whoever comes to me I will never drive away (Jn 6:37 NIV).

> And this is the testimony: God has given us eternal life, and this life is in his Son. He who has the Son has life; he who does not have the Son of God does not have life (1 Jn 5:11, 12 NIV).

> Here I am! I stand at the door and knock. If anyone hears my voice and opens the door, I will come in and eat with him, and he with me (Rev 3:20 NIV).

'So you've accepted Christ?' I enquired of a new believer.

'Yes, I did tonight.'

'And has he come into your life?'

'Well . . . I hope so.'

'But what does it say in his promise here in Revelation?' I persisted.

'It says "I will come in"'.

'So did he come in?' I felt like a schoolmaster.

'I suppose he must have.'

'Why?'

'Because he says so.'

It's a sure and safe ground of assurance—the Bible. We will learn more about this book of books in the next chapter. But come now to a second signpost that God really accepts the believer.

The work of Christ

Why do you suppose that followers of Jesus Christ are in the habit of receiving bread and wine together in the Holy Communion, or Lord's Supper? It is because we forget so easily! We need to be continually reminded that our Lord allowed his body to be broken and his blood to be shed on the cross for one tremendous purpose; namely, that our sins might be forgiven and that we might be brought to God. The bread and wine are like visual aids that tell the sinful, doubting believer again and again, *Yes, Christ loves you, accepts you, forgives you—the proof is in his death on your behalf.*

You see, we find it difficult to believe that we can be forgiven. The saving work of Christ upon the cross is a firm historical demonstration of his ability and desire to forgive.

'God has forgiven me *all* my sins', I once heard a new Christian declare enthusiastically. But what did he expect? That God would say 'I will forgive that sin, and that one, and possibly that misdemeanour...*but not this one I'm afraid*? Not at all! When God forgives, he forgives thoroughly. He adopts us into his family and makes us his own for ever.

'What about those daily sins that I continue to commit as a disciple?' I hear you ask. Try and get it clear; when we have been brought into the family of God, he is not going to cast us off. When our children were little, they would misbehave at times. Occasionally they might even break a window—*but they never ceased to be our children.*

The same with God. When we are brought into his family we learn that we are accepted; sins, habits and all. What do we do then about those daily wrongs, of which we become aware? We confess them, as children would to a father that they didn't want to hurt. I like the words that the apostle John wrote in his letter to people who were already Christians:

> If we confess our sins, he is faithful and just and will forgive us our sins and purify us from all unrighteousness (1 Jn 1:9 NIV).

How often I have come back to those words for reassurance! Behind them lies the massive truth of that great initial forgiveness that stems from the cross, and that covers us for now and always.

But let us look briefly at the third of those reassuring biblical Ws.

The witness of the Holy Spirit

This is something inward which we read of in the New Testament:

The Spirit himself testifies with our spirit that we are God's children (Rom 8:16 NIV).

'So,' you say, 'Christian assurance *is* to do with feelings after all.'

Not exactly. It is more to do with *experience*. As we advance in the life of the Spirit of Christ, we shall begin to experience touches of his transforming power in our character and lifestyle. At first it may be observers who can detect that we are different—we may be too close to the situation to assess ourselves. But changes there most certainly will be—if Christ has indeed taken over at the helm of the ship. What are these changes? Check yourself and see whether any of the following marks of the Christian are in you!

Do you find yourself beginning to respond to Christ's leadership; that you want to please him? Does it sadden you when you fail him? Do you find yourself beginning to move closer to others who belong to Jesus Christ? Are you aware of pressure or misunderstanding from those who reject his claims? Is it difficult, fighting against temptation and low standards? Does it hurt you when you hear Christ and his church being spoken against?

If the answer is Yes, then take heart; you have the witness of the Spirit within you!

The three Ws. You have realized by now that the three divine Persons of the Trinity act together to help the Christian onto a firm basis of assurance and confidence.

It is not presumptuous to think this way, because it is all of God and not of ourselves. Some Christians go through all of their pilgrimage in a mist of uncertainty. They truly belong to God's family, but they constantly worry about themselves and God. It is a pity if this is so, because they are unlikely to help many of their friends into a position of firm and confident belief— they are always worried about *themselves*.

This need not be so. The apostle John wrote his gospel for one purpose, and his New Testament letter for another. The gospel was written for unbelievers— 'that you may believe that Jesus is the Christ, the Son of God, and that by believing you may have life in his name' (Jn 20:31 NIV). But his letter was written for those who already believed ... for what purpose? Let John tell us:

> I write these things to you who believe in the name of the Son of God so that you may know that you have eternal life (1 Jn 5:13 NIV).

So that you may know ... Someone was once pouring cold water on the experience of a new Christian. 'In any case,' he challenged, 'how do you know that you're a Christian?'

The Christian didn't know too much, but she rose to the occasion. '*I was there when it happened!*' she retorted.

*   *   *   *

To learn: 1 John 5:11, 12 (That's the letter, not the gospel!)

Group work: Are you in a student group, confirmation class or beginners' meeting? You may like to study a Bible passage together, relating to these first two chapters. Try Luke 19:1–10. After praying for God's help in understanding the passage, read these ten verses, and then discuss the passage, using the following questions to stimulate the group:

1. Try and visualize the lifestyle of a tax collector like Zacchaeus. What sort of a person was he?

2. Why was this tax collector anxious to see Jesus? Can you think of various reasons? What fascinates people even today about Christ? What was your own experience?

3. What is the keynote that is stamped upon verse 5? (You may like to compare John 11:43.) What do we learn about Jesus from this verse?

4. Look at verse 6: 'gladly'. Why this reaction?

5. Compare the reaction of the onlookers in verse 7. What does this reaction tell us about the onlookers, about Zacchaeus and about Christ?

6. Discuss the changes that would have come into the life of Zacchaeus as a result of this encounter. How might these compare with twentieth-century experiences?

7. Verses 9 and 10—'Salvation...save...' What do these words mean? Can members of the group describe in their own words the basis, call and promise of salvation?

Ignorance of the Scriptures is ignorance of Christ
—JEROME
fourth-century Bible translator and scholar

3
God's Library

I was talking one Sunday night to a student, who had put his faith in Christ only a week or two earlier.

'And how about the Bible?' I enquired. 'Do you know much about it?'

'Look,' came the reply, 'all I know is that I've become a Christian. Apart from that I know *nothing*.'

When people tell me that, my heart pounds a little faster with excitement. If only they knew what was in store for them—the world of discovery that lay ahead! For it is the Bible that, to a large degree, has under-girded our civilization; has taught us about the value of the individual, the direction and purpose of history, the nature of man and the origin of the created order. But, more than anything else, it is the Bible that points us to Jesus Christ and builds us up in our relationship with him.

The Bible! What is it exactly?

'Oh,' you say, 'it's a book.'

Wrong! It's a *library* of books. Sixty-six of them, to be precise, written over a period of some fifteen hundred years by a wide range of individuals. Among the writers we can identify a general, a shepherd, a king, a farmer, a fisherman, a doctor and a taxman! Some library!

Correction. It's *two* libraries we're talking about—the Old and the New Testament; thirty-nine books in the Old and twenty-seven in the New. What is the common theme that links them?

It's Christ. Think of the biblical revelation from God as being shaped like an hour glass—or one of those old-fashioned egg-timers; wide at the two ends and narrow at the centre where the sand trickles through. Starting at the one end—Genesis—the hour glass is very wide. The concept is enormous—'God saw everything that he had made and it was good.' Creation and the universe.

Then we read, 'Let us make man in our image.' So this is a collection of books geared to meet the needs of *man.* But then we see a narrowing process as the Old Testament traces the fortunes of a single chosen *family*—that of Israel—through whom God chooses to work and to disclose his will for the world. One nation among many.

A further narrowing takes place, because Israel fails in her calling, and at a certain point some four-fifths of the nation go into captivity. We are then left with Judea, a tiny kingdom roughly the size of the English county of Yorkshire, or the diminutive American state of New Jersey. How the stage has shrunk!

It shrinks further still, because even that little remnant fails and goes into captivity. From it a still more reduced band is eventually restored. But even that minority is found unworthy to be God's instrument of redemption among the nations. So at the point when BC becomes AD the hour glass narrows to a tiny little band of just thirteen men—Jesus and the twelve. Could it get any smaller than that?

It could and does. The drama boils to a crisis, and even that tiny band comes apart, so that finally we are left with *one individual* who dies in solitary degradation. At that point, everything in the divine plan hangs upon him...a single grain of sand at the narrowest point.

From then on the widening begins again as Jesus, once-crucified and now reigning, sends his church out—to serve and evangelize with the good news into Jerusalem, Judea, Samaria...and out into a Gentile setting; Rome, Europe and the world.

You could sum up the major themes of the Bible, then, as the Creation; the revolt of mankind against God's rule; sin, evil and the need of reconciliation; the promised Saviour, foretold by the prophets; the saving work of Christ; the new community, the church, and the ultimate victory occasioned by the return of Christ.

That sounds like a lifetime of reading!

But why not? These two libraries of books are going to shape your life—and it may be that just now you know next to nothing about them! So let's make a start. Where do we begin? Genesis?

Probably not! Remember, we are dealing with two libraries, not a single book. We are not obliged to work our way through all sixty-six books consecutively. No, you and I are living on the AD side of history, so we will start with the life of Christ.

Beginning with Matthew? You don't have to. Why not start with Luke, a book written by a Gentile for Gentile readers? You'll love Luke—a warm, human, compassionate person who has helped millions fall in love with Jesus. And when you've read Luke's Gospel, read it again! Later you can move on to Matthew, Mark and John.

But remember, these are *gospels*, not biographies. Plenty of material is common to them all, of course, but each of them highlights different aspects of the person and work of Christ. They complement one another.

And after the Gospels? Maybe the Acts of the Apostles, where we see the developing life and ministry of the early Christian Church. Later on you can read some of Paul's letters to the young churches... Philippians   ...Ephesians...Colossians...Romans (that's the T-Bone steak!). Steadily get acquainted with the whole of the New Testament.

It's not too daunting. Why, the New Testament has about the same number of words as a single edition of the *New York Sunday Times*! It's infinitely smaller than many school books and university text books. I remember meeting an evangelist in Tanzania; his name was Zechariah Msonga. He was brought up as the son of a witch-doctor; he had never been to school. But how he knew his Bible! Somehow, in his eagerness to absorb the message of salvation, he had taught himself to read, and hundreds upon hundreds of his fellow-countrymen would gather to hear him share what he had learnt.

But what is so special about the Bible? Let it describe itself:

All Scripture is inspired by God and profitable for teaching, for reproof, for correction, and for training in righteousness, that the man of God may be complete, equipped for every good work (2 Tim 3:16, 17 rsv).

Down the centuries all the Christian churches have been agreed upon this point—that the Scriptures of the Old and New Testaments are the very word of God. Take, for example, the historic formularies of the Church of England: 'Holy Scripture containeth all things necessary to salvation: so that whatsoever is not read therein, nor may be proved thereby, is not to be required of any man, that it should be believed as an article of the Faith, or be thought requisite or necessary to salvation. In the name of the holy Scripture we do understand those canonical Books of the Old and New Testament, of whose authority was never any doubt in the Church' (Articles of Religion, No. VI). The language is antiquated—but it sums up the attitude of all the churches towards these 'canonical Books'.

Canonical? It's from a Greek word *Kanon,* meaning 'standard' or 'rule'. We may well ask ourselves, by what standard *did* the books of the Bible become regarded as Scripture inspired by God? Why were some books included and others excluded? Let's look at this—briefly!

The Canon or standard governing the Old Testament seems to be threefold.

1. *These books were uniformly recognized by Jesus Christ.* His witness is vital and decisive (e.g. Lk 16:17; Lk 24:44).

2. *These books were accepted by God's people.* Jesus had many controversies with the Scribes and Pharisees of his day—but not about the authority of the Old Testament Scriptures; on that, everyone was agreed!

3. *These books were recognized and referred to by the New Testament.* Hundreds of Old Testament allusions and quotations figure in the New Testament.

And what is the Canon of the New Testament? Once again, we come to Christ, the great authority.

1. *The New Testament books are Christ-centred in their*

content. You will see it again and again as you read for yourself.

2. *The New Testament books are apostolic in their authorship*. That is, they derive from the apostles—who received their authority from Christ. The apostles were themselves aware that God was speaking through them (1 Cor 2:12, 13). Peter at one point brackets Paul's letters with what he calls 'the other Scriptures' (2 Pet 3:16).

3. *The New Testament books are life-giving in their impact*. The new believers were told to have the books read in the churches (1 Thess 5:27). Why? Because these books make people more like Jesus Christ in character and lifestyle, and lead us to life in him (Jn 20:30–31).

So who put the books into the Bible? The true answer is that no one did. They put themselves in by the intrinsic quality that shone from their words. People read these books and they were blessed. The closing of the Canon finally came about during the fourth and fifth centuries AD. The two libraries are complete, and we are not to tamper with them or add to them (2 Cor 4:2; Rev 22:18, 19).

We must realize that it was no mere pronouncement by the Church that gave these books their authority. *This they already possessed*. I can look at a quality canvas and acclaim it as a genuine Monet. It is not my *saying* it that makes the painting genuine! By its own inherent power it has imposed itself upon me. It has been the same with the Scriptures. Men and women have read them—and they have met with God. They have fed upon the gospels and New Testament letters—and they have become more like Christ.

You and I must establish and develop our own approach to the reading of the Scriptures. Many Christians like to read in the morning, when they are fresh mentally. A good way to begin the day! Our reading will frequently shape the way in which we pray, for Bible reading and prayer tend to go together.

And why not daily? Choose your Bible carefully—but it need not be such a *de luxe* edition that you become afraid to use it. Expect to wear out your Bible every two or three years. And what version? If you can afford it, go for *two* editions; a reliable, standard *study* Bible, known for its accuracy (such as the Revised Standard Version), and a contemporary translation (such as the Good News Bible), one which is refreshing and uplifting in its sheer readability! You may even get the best of both worlds by obtaining the New International Version.

Don't bite off more than you can chew... but *do make a start*. Five minutes? Ten minutes? Half an hour? You will know what your appetite is like. Pray briefly before you read, with the firm expectation that God will instruct you through his two libraries, that he will inspire and lift you as a Christian. Will there be an example to follow in today's reading? A warning to heed? A truth to accept? A promise to claim? A spur to prayer?

Test yourself later in the day. *What was it I was reading? What was the key thought in the passage?* For it is Bible reading, combined with prayer, that shapes and affects our lives as Christians more than any other factor. We may not believe it when we hear it, but in five years' time, experience will have proved the point, more than you could have dreamed was possible!

* * * *

To learn: Try 2 Timothy 3:16, 17 this time. Remember to say the reference both before and after the sentence!

I want to say that I consider myself fortunate to be able to stand here and testify that I'm in the dock as a believer
— GEORGI VINS, ON TRIAL IN MOSCOW

4
Going Public

I can remember years ago when I was a teenager, a Christmas present arriving from my Aunt Carol. My aunt's presents were always very generous, but because of her busy life they sometimes weren't wrapped too carefully. On this occasion she had sent our family a magnificent bagatelle set—but even as it arrived, we could see that it would be some time before we could use it. As the postman brought the parcel to the door, the last of the little silver balls dropped out!

Everyone knows the experience of not being able to use a new possession. The dress that has to be hemmed up before it can be worn; the gadget that needs a battery before it can be switched on. But what of the new life that comes to us in Jesus Christ? Can it be put to use in the service of God from the outset, or is some extra accessory required before we can go public?

Going public is what is meant by the biblical term 'witness'. We receive God's pardon and his assurance of friendship, and then become public 'witnesses' to his generosity and love. It's a term of the law courts— we are in the dock and are required to give witness of what we know. In many parts of the world this is literally the case—the believer may have to stand trial, simply for being a Christian. In this century thousands upon thousands of our fellow-believers have faced prison sentences and the firing-squad. They were witnesses to Christ.

And so are we! In a variety of ways we are to show which side we are on, to declare ourselves unashamedly, and share with others what we have experienced in Christ. We are going public. But how is this best done, and how long am I to wait before I can begin? Do I need a special power pack first?

We witness for God immediately

Terrifying as it may sound, we can start at once. No, we do not need to wait for a further power boost, as those apostles of Jesus did when their Master ascended from their view. Then, certainly, they had to wait for the coming of the Holy Spirit to empower the whole Church. This happened in Jerusalem within a few weeks. But from then on, the gift of the Holy Spirit was an integral part of the great gospel offer—remember? *Two gifts*; forgiveness *and* the Holy Spirit! If we belong to Christ at all, then his Spirit indwells us:

> …If anyone does not have the Spirit of Christ, he does not belong to Christ (Rom 8:9 NIV).

We must understand that the power of the Spirit of Christ is at work within us from the first moment of our response to him. There is no reason why we should not witness for God immediately.

We witness for God naturally

Speech, attitudes, friendships, work—in a dozen different ways it will begin to emerge that there is a new dimension in the life of a Christian. Let us not for a moment think that this means *reduction* in the things we are doing outside of the church. Christianity is not a new club, a new craze! No, as far as the home, the college course, the business career are concerned, I am not talking about reduction but *enhancement*.

Learn from the mistaken view illustrated in this imaginary conversation between Colin, a high flyer who is rising to prominence in his firm, and his boss:

Boss: 'There's one hesitation we have about you, Colin. Before we can offer you the new section in our overseas operation, we would want to be assured that your commitment to us was one hundred per cent. How do you feel?'

Colin: 'I believe I could handle the new section. I hope my commitment is strong enough.'

Boss: 'You say, I hope. Frankly, we're not sure that your energies aren't more soaked up in your new Christian business lunch activities. Not that I've any quarrel with Christianity, of course. But I must be honest with you and say that we would want to be satisfied about your single-minded commitment to us if this post is going to come your way.'

Colin: 'Oh well, of course, I must be quite clear that my Christian interests mean more to me than anything. My *real* commitment lies in that direction. That always comes first now.'

Boss: 'Thanks for being open with me, Colin. That confirms the impression one or two of us had gained about you. It means—if I can be equally frank—that we ought to offer the new section to someone else. I'm sure you understand that in such a vital development we've got to be absolutely sure about the new man's commitment. Thanks for coming; see you later.'

What a pity! I sympathize with the boss—of course he wanted a full-blooded commitment to the company. *And he would have had it, if Colin had properly understood that Christian commitment affects the whole of life,* and can never be pushed into a 'religious' compartment of its own. As a Christian, Colin should have been able to assure his boss that he was indeed one hundred per cent ambitious to be in the right place and to exercise as great an influence as possible on the way the company was run. His Christian commitment should have enhanced the contribution he could make to his firm. Pity!

The apostle Paul told even the slaves of the Roman era that, as Christians, they could now work with a new zest!

> Slaves, obey your earthly masters in everything; and do it, not only when their eye is on you and to win their favour, but with sincerity of heart and reverence for the Lord. Whatever you do, work at it with all your heart, as working for the Lord, not for men...(Col 3:22, 23 NIV).

It is Christ who gives this new quality to work, to relationships, to leisure, home and the family. It is bound to surface as a daily witness to him—naturally.

We witness for God personally

I once remember seeing an evangelist standing on a box at the side of a great thoroughfare. Amid the deafening traffic he was doing his best to explain the Christian faith from a large Bible that he was holding. Nobody was paying him the slightest attention. Admiring his courage, I went and stood for a while in front of his box trying to look as 'many' as possible!

Yes, there is a place for that kind of thing; indeed we send teams from our own London church of All Souls, Langham Place to preach and witness in busy Oxford Circus. But such an approach is a somewhat artificial way of witnessing. It is certainly not the most effective.

The most effective way of all is through personal friendship. There is absolutely no doubt about it. We want to witness to the truth and light that centres in Jesus Christ? What better way than among relatives and friends whom we already know? It may be hard, because we live among them—there is little escape! But the rightness of such witness is irrefutable. We read in the New Testament of one man who, freed from his past, begged to follow Christ. He wanted to join in the great crusade:

> Jesus did not let him, but said, 'Go home to your family and tell them how much the Lord has done for you...' (Mk 5:19 NIV).

Your public witness may not be with words at first. A changed life and attitude is worth any number of home-produced sermons! I like the words of the apostle Peter: 'Always be prepared to give an answer to everyone who asks you to give the reason for the hope that

you have. But do this with gentleness and respect...'
(1 Pet 3:15 NIV).

This kind of thing can be rehearsed. At some point
you are going to be asked about your beliefs, your
outlook. Keep on the watch for those natural opportu-
nities. Don't force them or start 'working round' to the
subject of your faith—people soon learn to run a mile
from peddlers of an obsession. Simply be ready to
share, in humility, what in your limited understanding
you have learnt of Christ. Think it out...how you
would say it... your reasons...your discoveries. You
are not there to pronounce on philosophical profun-
dities; frequently you will be unable to give a single
answer to your critics—you are a beginner! But at
least, like the man healed by Jesus, you will be able to
say, 'One thing I do know. I was blind but now I see!'
(Jn 9:25 NIV).

We witness for God publicly

There are many ways of making a public affirmation of
faith. Many times I have interviewed members of our
church during a worship service—it is a way of helping
them to declare themselves as well as imparting a
challenge to others. Sometimes people have registered
their decision to follow Christ by stepping forward at
the close of a crowded mission service, to seek prayer
and counsel. But there is one way of going public that
should be common to every believer—*and that is to take
your baptism seriously.*

Baptism...this is *the* outward distinguishing mark
of the Christian. It signifies a farewell to the old life
and an introduction to the new. It dramatizes the
inward washing from sin, made available by the death

of Jesus. It identifies the one baptized as someone for
whom Christ came in love—to forgive and to regener-
ate with his Spirit. We recall the farewell words of our
Master:

> All authority in heaven and on earth has been given to
> me. Therefore go and make disciples of all nations,
> baptising them in the name of the Father and of the Son
> and of the Holy Spirit…(Mt 28:18, 19 NIV).

So Christian baptism, instituted by Jesus Christ, is
one of the two great 'sacraments' of the gospel (the
Holy Communion being the other). It is a powerful
outward symbol (water) of an inward and spiritual
reality (cleansing from sin). It is always applied in the
name of the Trinity, and it is something that every true
church takes seriously.

'Ah,' you say, 'I haven't been baptized.'

Fine, you can be. If, as a Christian, you are now
linked with a church, make sure that you talk with the
leaders and seek their advice. Without any doubt they
will have their own arrangements for Christian
baptism and for the necessary preparation.

'Ah,' you say, 'I was baptized as a baby.' Good. And
better still, now that you are a believer! You evidently
come from an Anglican or Episcopal church background. Entering into the inward reality of forgiveness
and new life has now *completed* your baptism.

Infant baptism, then, or believers' baptism? We do
not have to quarrel between our church traditions
over the mode of baptism, nor indeed over the amount
of water used! In recent years responsible Christians
have learnt to refrain from attacking or converting one
another over Christ's wonderful ordinance of baptism.

Provided that inward personal faith at some point completes the baptism, we may feel deeply privileged to be carrying this invisible mark of the Lord.

Of course, Christian experience is often untidy. Sometimes a person is baptized as an adult, only to enter into an experience of Christ later on. Is there a need to be baptized again? No, certainly not; the same principle holds as with infant baptism—the initiation should now be seen as a completed entity.

Some reading this book will have been baptized in infancy and, having come to faith, are now heading towards confirmation—when the promises made on your behalf as an infant are now publicly adopted and ratified by yourself. That is your own church's domestic arrangement of helping you to 'go public', and so take your baptism seriously. Other readers will have been 'dedicated', perhaps in infancy, and are now thinking carefully about being baptized. Whatever the pattern, may God help every one of us who has begun with Christ to be bold and unashamed in our public testimony for him.

I remember a senior citizen in our own church who was ready to go public in a confirmation service. I asked her to fill in a form, so that the church register could be completed properly. In the section headed 'Details of your date and place of baptism', she had written, 'Baptism certificate destroyed by enemy action in 1940.'

It didn't matter! To quote another lady, Gladys Aylward, famous for her Christian work in China: 'God won't ask you for certificates; he'll only ask if you've been faithful to your call.'

*   *   *   *

To learn: Romans 1:16.

Group work: Try this study together—Matthew 5:11–16. After a brief prayer for God's help in understanding the Scriptures, read the passage, and then use the following questions to stimulate discussion:

1. Verse 11 rounds off what are called 'The Beatitudes' from Christ's sermon on the mount, with their description of a new kind of 'blessedness' or happiness. What is so revolutionary and different about the happiness that Christ gives? What is the group's experience?

2. Verses 11 and 12 speak of adversity and opposition. Has this been anyone's experience to date? How should we react to such difficulties? How may we be best prepared for them?

3. Verse 13—salt. Why does Jesus Christ use this word to describe the influence of Christians? In what way does this sentence correct us when we are inclined to retreat from society and its pressures? Can you think of Christians who have used their influence for God in wider circles?

4. What is the warning for us in verse 13? What causes Christian people to lose their 'different' quality and to become identical with the world around?

5. Look at verses 14 and 15. What is the value of this description of Christ's followers? What is the main force of meaning here? How can we avoid the ostentation of, say, the Pharisees of Christ's time; and more closely resemble Christ, as we try to live out these verses? Verse 16 may help.

6. What are the biggest mistakes we have tended to make in this matter of 'witnessing'? How can we learn from them?

7. What was the main factor that first helped *you* to become a follower of Christ? A book? The friendship of a Christian? Family upbringing? What can be learnt from the group's experiences?

PART TWO

The Body-Builders

A Christian is not of hasty growth, like a mushroom, but rather like the oak, the progress of which is hardly perceptible, but, in time, becomes a great deep-rooted tree.

John Newton, in a letter, June 1776

He is not a hero to be admired or an ideal to be followed; He is a friend, who in the relationship of friendship both speaks and acts. He speaks, we hear; we speak, He hears. There is genuine fellowship and exchange.

—STEPHEN NEILL

5

The Baobab and the Vine

'Do you think you could stop the car?' I asked. 'I can see a baobab tree and I have an urge to photograph it.'

Bob Glen, a missionary friend from New Zealand, was driving me through Tanzania's scrubby terrain on an African trip. Obligingly he brought the Volkswagen to a halt, and I dug out the camera. You see, I've always had a fascination for baobabs.

I must have caught this from my father. He was for ever stopping by baobab trees, gazing at them, measuring them and photographing them. Incredibly thick and gnarled, they are a phenomenon of hardy growth in the arid African bush, somehow retaining enough moisture in their sturdy trunks to keep going.

We who have begun with Christ do well to reflect on the many instances there are of survival and growth in alien conditions. There is the baobab tree of Tanzania, the edelweiss flower of the Swiss Alps…and there is the Christian believer of God's world. Yes, it *is* God's world—and yet it is a world in revolt, scorched by conflict and revolution, levelled off by the inexorable advance of secularization. Society seems to have closed off the sky, and we find ourselves pitched into a waterless plain. And then we are told to grow...

Let the expectations remain high! For a further piece of imagery encourages us at this point. Not the baobab tree so much as the Vine:

> Abide in me and I in you. As the branch cannot bear fruit by itself, unless it abides in the vine, neither can you, unless you abide in me. I am the vine, you are the branches. He who abides in me, and I in him, he it is that bears much fruit, for apart from me you can do nothing (Jn 15:4, 5 RSV).

Christ's words should give a lift to every believer who wishes to be 'fruitful'—that is, to grow in character and effective Christian service. Invisibly, we are joined to our Master. We thought, on receiving his Spirit into our lives, that he was in us. But in this amazing concept of union with Christ, we may also think of ourselves as in him! It's not too difficult to grasp. Throw a sponge in the bath water—is the sponge in the water, or the water in the sponge?

It is this union with Christ that accounts for the way in which Christian growth perseveres, even in the most unpromising of circumstances. I'll never forget Ivan. Ivan was a young man from Romford, who wandered into our hall at St. Peter's Church, Harold Wood in Essex, when I was leading the work there some years ago.

'When's the dance beginning?' asked Ivan.

'Dance? There's no dance here; this is a Bible study. You can come to it if you like!'

And with that, the young man from a nominal Jewish background joined in the proceedings. Not that his Bible reading was up to much; in fact he couldn't read at all. Until a church member taught him to read, we would see Ivan at worship, book upside down, coping as cheerfully as he could with the hymns! He became a believer, and we watched the miracle of growth taking place in his life. Little by little the lifestyle that had periodically got him into trouble with the police began to alter. How hard it was! None of his friends or family had the slightest sympathy for his Christian stance. He got to know what it was to be thrown out, beaten up and disowned.

But Christ was at work in his life, and we loved him.

What causes a person to grow in this way? What principles operate? 'How', a new Christian may be asking, 'can I make a success of this Christianity business and become more like Jesus Christ?' Let's look at a few guidelines.

Growth is not sudden but progressive

Christian growth can't happen overnight. Of course the start can happen in an instant. The moment we respond to the good news by repentance and faith—Click!—it's as instantaneous as the taking of a photograph. God accepts us into his family, forgiving us and entering our lives by his Spirit. Freely!

> They are justified by his grace as a gift, through the redemption which is in Christ Jesus (Rom 3:24 RSV).

God has declared us as righteous, just people (although we are still very bad). We call this unique truth *justification*. It is the start. But progressing as a Christian, and becoming actually more like Christ in outlook and character—this takes time. The process of becoming holy is called *sanctification*:

For this is the will of God, your sanctification: that you abstain from unchastity…(1 Thess 4:3, 4 RSV).

Justification happens initially and in an instant. Sanctification happens gradually, progressively and sometimes painfully. When you were justified you were declared righteous. In being sanctified, however, you are made righteous. Justification is like the *click*, the initial snapping of the photograph. Sanctification is like the *processing*, the developing of the film. It takes a lifetime! It is not sudden but progressive.

Growth is not mechanical but personal

It is not a matter of technique, this process of growing as a Christian. It is a *relationship*. It's not like learning Hindustani! Becoming like Jesus Christ in character and life could never be a business of getting through the right number of prayers, adopting the correct posture for worship, or reciting mantras into the night. Jesus told us that this was the way of the unbelieving heathen (Mt 6:7), who think that they will be heard for their many words. Christ is no mere guru. And we are not mere devotees, learning a system. Jesus' words should warm the hearts of all who love him:

I have called you friends (Jn 15:15 RSV).

Christianity on the personal level is a partnership, a daily adventure with a living Friend. We have entered into a developing relationship with someone we have never seen! The words of the apostle Peter find an echo in the experience of millions: 'Without having seen him you love him; though you do not now see him you believe in him and rejoice with unutterable and exalted joy' (1 Pet 1:8 RSV). As one new believer once put it to me: 'If Jesus told me now to go and jump in the lake, I'd do it!'

Of course, the relationship must be developed, following the individual's initial encounter with Christ. In this it resembles a marriage. It would be a strange wedding if, at the end of the reception, the bridegroom were to say to his bride: 'It's been a great day! Thank you ever so much for marrying me. The ceremony, the cake, the confetti—I loved every minute of it... Well, maybe we'll meet again one day!' A relationship needs plenty of practice.

Somebody once coined the phrase 'Practising the presence of God.' I don't know that I really like this description of Christian discipline—it reminds me too much of a technique or ritual. But the intention behind it is important. We are going to need perpetual reminders of our unseen Companion. We shall rely— baobab-like—on the resources he makes available to us through prayer and the Bible. Ours is a walk of faith. The opposite of faith is *sight*! We cannot see Christ. There is no hot-line word of mouth communication from him to us. No telex messages.

'*We walk by faith, not by sight*' (2 Cor 5:7 RSV). True, ours is a reasonable faith—it is not a blind leap into the dark. We have been persuaded by the data available to us that God is there, that he loves us in his Son Jesus Christ, and that the Good Shepherd has indeed become *my* Shepherd. But we are still not going to see him. Not this side of the grave. All that we shall receive from him by way of resources and spiritual strength will be *mediated* to us. This is where prayer and the Bible come into their own. Of course, this takes prac-

tice—and effort! Which leads us to a third guideline
for the developing of the relationship.

Growth is not passive but strenuous

This cannot be ignored. We are humans, not puppets.
All the way through it is God who graciously takes the
initiative, revealing himself to us in Christ, giving us
his message of truth in the Bible, putting us into his
church. But we are required to co-operate. Victory
over evil is promised to us, *if we are willing to resist sin*. It
is not all one-way. We can apply this to guidance.

God's guidance comes to us, as Christians, for the
running of our lives. It comes through the great principles of the Bible (he will never guide us to do something
that is contrary to his revealed word); it comes to us
through the promptings of the Holy Spirit in our
prayers; it comes to us through the way in which our
circumstances are shaped; it comes to us through the
advice of our Christian friends and leaders. Here again,
it does not, for the most part, get handed to us on a
plate. No telex messages as to where we are to take our
holiday! *Reason*: we are not puppets. Our intelligence,
will and decision-making abilities are all to be called
into play. 'I will instruct you and teach you the way
you should go', comes the message of Psalm 32:8. 'I
will counsel you with my eye upon you.' A great
promise of guidance and leadership! But read on...

Be not like a horse or a mule, without understanding,
which must be curbed with bit and bridle...(Ps 32:9
RSV).

So Christian growth and discipleship do not just

happen while we remain passive onlookers. Our own unique individuality is not going to get ironed out as God takes over the leadership of our lives. Rather, our energies will become enhanced and exercised in wrestling to understand what the Bible is saying to us, fighting against temptation, deciding as Christians again and again on numerous options that are open to us—the promotion, the mortgage, the holiday, finance, marriage and the family. The apostle Paul expresses this well in Philippians 2:12, 13 (RSV) '...work out your own salvation with fear and trembling; for God is at work in you, both to will and to work for his good pleasure.' The life of salvation has already been given to us freely. *Now we are to work it out,* applying it in the arena of daily living—but always with the reassuring knowledge that the resources and power behind us and within us are from God.

Growth is not passive. Nobody else is going to run our lives for us. Not for us the strange authoritarian groups and churches that like to sanction your every decision. We shall always be glad of the advice and leadership of more experienced Christians—but we are not disciples of *them*. We are disciples of one Man only! One last guideline.

Growth is not private but corporate

Let's emphasize it again: Real Christianity can never be a solitary esoteric weekend pursuit, a private affair of self-improvement, assisted by books, night-school and personal tutors. We have been born into a family, an astounding assortment of badly-matched personalities, eccentrics and misfits. *You are one of them.*

And this church is no mere club. Privacy, you see, is

out. How terrifying! As Christ's new community, we shall be called to give our service to an unfriendly world, to identify with it, to penetrate it with our own distinctive world-view, to battle with its prejudices and to engage in its debates. In doing so, we shall undoubtedly get buffeted...but this is part of the growing process. Gifts and abilities will get stretched to the full, in the service of our leader—and with one joint aim:

> ...until we all attain to the unity of the faith and of the knowledge of the Son of God, to mature manhood, to the measure of the stature of the fullness of Christ; so that we may no longer be children, tossed to and fro and carried about with every wind of doctrine...(Eph 4:13, 14 RSV)

It is a joint, a corporate goal. You are not on your own. Frequently we shall find that Christian growth is something that rubs off, from one to the other. You and I may not be able to assess our own personal progress; others will be able to observe us better than we can ourselves. What we are required to do is to focus—not upon ourselves, but upon Christ. *There* is our standard!

An impossible goal? Bertrand Russell, the atheist philosopher, commented on Christianity: 'There is nothing to be said against it, except that it is too difficult for most of us to practise sincerely.' A masterly understatement! It is not simply difficult; it is impossible. Then why did we ever start?

Let John Newton, author of 'Amazing Grace' and many other great hymns, state the case. A blaspheming slave trader in earlier life, he became, after his conversion to Christ, an outstanding pastor and evangelist. He once said: *'I am not what I ought to be; I am not what I wish to be; I am not what I hope to be; but, by the grace of God, I am not what I was!'*

Take a second look at those words of New Testament experience. They will find an echo in every struggling —and growing—believer!

*   *   *   *

To learn: Try Philippians 1:6. Then see if you can remember the four other scripture passages memorized so far.

. . . Just as the Party is the plausibility structure for Marxism, and the Senior Common Room can be the same for secular humanism, the Church is the plausibility structure for the Christian faith. . . . The Church is Christianity's working model, its pilot plant, its future in embryo

— Os Guinness

6

The Working Model

'It's going to be the picture of the year', said my brother Peter.

There were six of us in the group, posing in front of the beautiful Swiss mountains, the Eiger, the Münch and the Jungfrau. It was the ideal spot for our family Christmas card photograph; there were the three peaks, the snow and a chalet. There may even have been a cow—I forget.

'Eight seconds to go!' The automatic timing device in the camera was set up in motion as my brother dashed over to take his place in the group. Six faces froze in a grin. A click. It was in the bag...Switzerland at its best.

Calamity. Several weeks later we saw the result. At the moment of exposure some perspiring oaf of an English tourist had casually walked up behind our group; the camera had caught him looking over our shoulders into the lens, cigarette in mouth, knotted handkerchief on his head and wearing braces! Not the best image of a beautiful country. We had to find an alternative.

This is the problem of the ad-men, of promoters and

propagandists, of politicians and ideologists—how to present the best possible image to their consumers. But it is your problem and mine too, if we have any concern for the impression that an unbelieving world is going to gain of Christ.

Jesus Christ...the most perfect being that ever walked the hills and valleys of our world, the flawless reflection of the divine Father. There had never been anyone like him before his arrival, and no one since has even approached his purity and stature. But how is his living presence to be expressed among humanity? Incredibly, it is through the church. It is all part of God's plan.

> He has put all things under his feet and has made him the head over all things for the church, which is his body, the fullness of him who fills all in all (Eph 1:22, 23 RSV).

It is a breathtaking concept. Christians are the company of people that Christ has called out to follow himself ('church' in the Greek simply means those 'called out'). To no other body of people has the Son of God pledged his presence. Get any group of believers together, big or small, and we can be sure that Christ is there among them by his Spirit to 'fill' them with his presence.

But we are to be Christ's 'fullness' too! Think about it a moment. The world's concept of Jesus Christ is amazingly deficient. The popular image of God's Messiah is frequently distorted. Yes, if someone takes the trouble to read the Bible, they can obtain a marvellous portrait of Jesus, but they still need to 'see' him in flesh and blood terms.

The picture needs filling out. That's your cue and

mine. It is up to us, who have been called out and filled, to make Christ *visible* to as many people as possible. Os Guinness describes the church as Christianity's 'plausibility structure' (*The Gravedigger File*, Hodder). Let me illustrate this idea.

I remember meeting a young Belgian woman of twenty-five in Brussels, during a Bible youth event. During her private search for God she had read the Bible for herself, and had accepted Christ into her life. But had she been taken for a ride? Was Christ and Christianity all make-believe—just a beautiful story? Françoise determined to find out if there were any others who shared her experience of Christ. For a long time she met with failure!

She approached the 'Jehovah's Witnesses' sect, but left them after a very short while. 'It was immediately apparent to me that they knew nothing of this new birth that I had received', she explained. She then joined the Mormon group of the 'Latter Day Saints', and was even married, by arrangement, to one of their leaders for a period—but left their ranks eventually, similarly disillusioned and inwardly scarred. Next she tried 'The Children of God', but discovered that their lifestyle bore little relationship to their public propaganda. They were not *plausible*, and she broke away from the authoritarianism of David Moses.

Françoise battled on. She met up with the Scientology movement, paying the full fee that was required of her for membership; but a similar disillusionment set in, and she finally severed her links with the sect, and continued her search for people who had a similar experience to her own. How hard it was! How many competing voices! She joined the ranks of the Guru Maharaj Ji, and stayed with the organization's devotees for a full year, but finally concluded bitterly that their leader was a false prophet, and she quit.

After a great deal of travelling and searching she returned home, and found that in her absence her own brother had also accepted Christ—and had joined a church! It was simply a traditional group of worshipping Christians. They were very ordinary people. They made no vast, extravagant claims. But they shared an experience of Christ in their lives. That was enough. Françoise's search was over!

And there she was in that youth event in Brussels, one of a truly motley crew. There were Baptists and Methodists; Presbyterians, Lutherans and Brethren; Anglicans and Moravians...eight thousand of us from thirty-nine different countries and from innumerable different traditions and Christian denominations—but Françoise felt at home among us, because we shared a common experience of Jesus. We recognized each other as members of the one body of Christ in spite of all our different emphases. *It was plausible.*

So what are we talking about, when we think of the church? Let's establish four brief points.

The church's necessity

If we are called out as Christians to make Christ known to the world and to express his living presence in a convincing way, then the church is no optional extra for the believer! It is easy to ridicule the more institutional aspects of the church, and to imagine that we can get along very well without it.

'You don't have to go to church to become a Christian', we hear. True. Françoise was a case in point. She found Christ on her own. But it is actually not possible to *be* a Christian, while remaining aloof from Christ's called-out body. If, of course, Jesus had come to found a new *philosophy*, then perhaps we could be excused for thinking that faith was a matter to be practised privately. But Jesus' purpose was very different. He came to found a new *community*! It was to be a community founded on faith in himself, as proclaimed by Peter and the other apostles:

> And I tell you, you are Peter, and on this rock I will build my church, and the powers of death shall not prevail against it (Mt 16:18 RSV).

In New Testament terms, then, the church is not that structure at the end of the road, with a noticeboard outside. That simply keeps the rain off the church! For the church of Christ is *people*. It is the Church Universal, composed of all races and languages; and it is the Church Local. It is vital to the Christian. We cannot afford to be like the man who wanted to join the navy, but who refused to be assigned to any particular ship!

The church's unity

This is a marvellous reality. We sense it when we go abroad and meet Christians of other cultures and traditions. There is a look in the eye, a similarity of expression; we can feel the vibrations...we are one!

Not that we never experience disunity. It is a tragedy of history that at times people supposedly following Jesus have, in their fallenness, criticized, attacked and even killed one another. Christ himself prophesied that such things would happen, and shortly before his death prayed for the new community that was to come into being:

> I pray also for those who will believe in me through their
> message, that all of them may be one, Father, just as you
> are in me and I am in you (Jn 17:20, 21 NIV).

There is evidently to be this family likeness among
Christians, a unity that is to reflect the union of heaven
itself, a unity that is to centre in the truth of Christ's
message. Such a unity is no mere *coalition* of unwilling
partners, forced together by pressure or accident; it is
a unity of disciples, drawn together by the unique
objective truth of God in Christ. Throughout the
centuries we have had to work at this, and it is no small
thing that the mainline churches are agreed upon the
great facts of the faith as summed up in the historic
creeds. It is a unity to be worked at—and maintained!

The church's diversity

But is the unity, written of above, *uniformity*? It cannot
be. Think of the early Christians. Jewish believers
were very different from Gentile believers. The
churches to which the apostle Paul addressed his letters
were all different from one another. There were differences in emphasis, in needs, in custom and in church
government.

But there were no differences in the *essentials*. You
can be different in liturgy, tradition, music, baptismal
discipline and millennial belief—and still have unity!
What chiefly tears the churches apart are not different
traditions, but a different *spirit*; the competitive
superiority that excludes a group of believers from
fellowship, unrecognized and unloved. *That offends
deeply*.

Is it *unanimity* we are after then? Again no. We do not

have to be agreed on every point. It is enough that we take the Scriptures as our authority, that we acknowledge Jesus as Lord, and that we baptize in the name of the Trinity. Where this happens, you have a church— even if you do not have unanimity on every point!

It will never be a perfect church. Realize this, and we can live with the tension. Accept this, and we can avoid the sectarian tendency of dismissing out of hand those who may differ from us. We have heard these voices all too often down the ages: *Join us! . . . Leave your churches . . . separate yourselves, you're not real believers . . . Come over to us out here in the wilderness . . . The truth is here!* The way of the sects, and of the successive splinter groups dividing to achieve an ever-greater purity, is the way of death. Membership of the body of Christ calls, not so much for uniformity or unanimity, as for *mutual recognition*. We are members of one family, and we are—in Christ—to accept each other as such, wherever we meet, and in particular at the Table of the Holy Communion.

The church's plausibility

Back to our starting point. The church—your church—is here to stay. It is placed in the world in order that it may fill out the picture of Jesus Christ for all of society, and make him real. We do this together as we worship, learn, serve and witness—doing all in our power to place our Lord unmistakably at the very, very centre of our life and fellowship.

Of course we will fail, again and again! The image of Christ that we present to our friends and neighbours will not always be very attractive. Sometimes we feel hampered by the creaking antiquity of it all. The

church at times resembles an old, old car. The tyres
are somewhat worn, the exhaust pipe rattles and the
steering is shaky. It's hardly surprising; a glance at the
dashboard shows that the figure of two thousand is
rapidly coming up on the clock—we've been on the
road a long time! But see how the Bible describes us:

> …the household of God, which is the church of the living
> God, the pillar and bulwark of the truth (1 Tim 3:15
> RSV).

What a role! So be in love with your church. There is
no alternative. It will never be perfect, however much
we can improve and change it, because you and I
happen to be among its members. Sometimes tensions
may arise within its ranks. Worry not! The New Testament body of Christ knew similar tensions. Indeed, if
you are in a church where there are no tensions, it is
not a church at all. It is a corpse!

*   *   *   *

To learn: Matthew 16:18.

Group work: After a brief prayer, read John 15:1–17.
The following may serve as discussion points:

1. What is this passage basically about? Try and
understand why Jesus spoke in these terms to his
followers.

2. In what way is the picture of a vine an apt symbol
for the church of Jesus Christ? What other symbols
can the group discover? *Clues:* Ephesians 1:22, 23;
2:19–22; 5:25–27.

3. Discuss from this passage the ways in which an individual grows as a Christian. What does it mean to 'abide' or 'remain' in Christ? How is this done, in the group's experience?

4. What part does the second half of verse 2 have to play in the development of the Christian? To what does this pruning process refer?

5. There are three instances in this passage in which Christ's words or commandments are said to help us. Can you find them, and identify the particular areas of our lives which benefit?

6. How often does the word 'fruit' occur? In practical terms what does this refer to?

7. How many 'relationship' phrases can be found, which describe our position in regard to Jesus Christ? Which is the strongest of these words or phrases?

We hold our common assembly on the day of the sun, because it is the first day, on which God put to flight darkness and chaos and made the world, and on the same day Jesus Christ our saviour rose from the dead

—Justin Martyr, c. ad 150

7

Surprised by Sunday

It was Sunday that originally gave me my love of avocado pears. We actually grew them at the first home that I can really remember, on the lower slopes of Mount Kenya. How often I recall starting off a new tree! With immense difficulty you insert a matchstick right through the hard kernel of an avocado; the shiny brown thing is then suspended over a vase, half in and half out of the water. That is just the start. It never occurred to me to ask how wild avocados could manage without vases and matchsticks—this was simply our way. Seven years later the resulting tree would produce its first fruit.

Being in somewhat short supply, avocados tended to be a Sunday speciality—as were other features of our urban-free existence. Sunday was my *papier mâché* day, my day with plywood and fretsaw, my painting and paper-chain day, my launching pad into the world of printing and potato-cuts. We also went to church.

I never did those things on other days. Sunday was different.

Have you discovered Sunday yet? Maybe you're in for a surprise. Cliff Richard was a comparatively new

Christian when he was performing in *Cinderella* at the London Palladium, years back. He was asked at that time:

'What is your favourite thing at the moment?'

'Sundays', he answered simply.

And why not? There is something about the principle of one day in seven that is woven deep into our created order. As early as Genesis chapter 2 it became established—long before the giving of the Ten Commandments and the Law. *One day in seven*; it is what Bible students call a 'creation ordinance'—it's basic to life and to existence.

At times, society has tampered with this pattern, but humanity suffers as a result. After the French Revolution, the task of drawing up a new republican calendar was entrusted to Charles Gilbert Romme, assisted by a bunch of able mathematicians. From September 1792, the year was to be divided into twelve months of thirty days each, every month being divided into three periods of ten days. These were called *décades*, the last day of each of these new 'weeks' being a day of rest. What happened? It didn't work! The scheme was officially abandoned on January 1st, 1806. Moral: don't fiddle around with creation ordinances!

Sunday can be an exciting discovery for the Christian believer. As a member of the acting profession said to me once, 'I find it better than roast beef and Yorkshire pudding.' The one day in seven is a precious gift.

Prize it

Learn to look forward to this special day—it's part of the order for the running of the world. It represents a break in the monotony of daily life. It is instituted for the good, not simply of religious people, but for man in general, as Christ reminded his listeners (Mk 2:27).

'Ah,' said one argumentative person to me once, 'You church people ought still to be worshipping on the Saturday; surely you're disobeying the Bible by making Sunday your special day!'

'But nowhere in my Bible,' I replied stoutly, 'am I told that I must set aside the seventh day *of the week*. Certainly it worked like that for the Jewish people, but look at the wording of the fourth commandment!' And I pointed it out:

> Six days you shall labour, and do all your work; but the seventh day (i.e. after six days of labour) is a sabbath to the Lord your God (Ex 20:9,10 RSV).

That is the principle; six days of work and routine—and then the rest day. It's basic to creation. But why, you may wonder, *did* the new Christian church change the habit of centuries, and substitute Sunday for Saturday? An early Christian document (AD 70–100) by Barnabas of Alexandria (no relation to St. Paul's companion) sums it up for us all: *Wherefore we keep the Lord's day with joyfulness, the day also on which Jesus rose from the dead.* Other early writers wrote in similar vein, and towards the end of the second century, Clement, also of Alexandria, and Christianity's first real scholar, was able to write, 'The old sabbath day has become no more than a working day.'

But even in New Testament times, there were hints of the new Christian Sunday: 'On the first day of the week, when we were gathered together to break bread ...' (Acts 20:7 RSV). What had happened? *Sunday had become enhanced.* It was God's day—the day of creation; it was the Lord's day—the day of resurrection and victory; it was the Spirit's day—the day of Pentecost, when the new Christian Church became infused with life. In a wonderful way Sunday is associated with the three Persons of the Trinity.

Across the centuries of Israel's history, the Sabbath had deteriorated into a day of regulations and solemn duties; it was Jesus who set it free, enhanced it, and gave it the extra dimensions of mercy and service. And then, when he rose from the dead, the day took on the aspect of a celebration. It is on *Sunday*—not simply Easter—that we celebrate the victory of Jesus as Lord. In the days of the Roman Empire, the Christian Sunday acted as a direct challenge to the claim that Caesar was Lord! In no lesser way should we esteem this wonderful day in our week.

Plan it

As I look back, I can see that a good deal of planning went into those early Sundays in Kenya, cut off as we were from shops, electricity, gas, running water, public transport and the telephone. Our pleasures were simple—and quite a number of them, I now realize, happened on Sunday…new clothes…avocados…special activities…tea with Auntie Lorna.

Lorna Bowden was a single woman, a missionary of uncertain age, who lived about a hundred yards away. But to our young legs a visit to her house was an excursion! She would do us proud on those Sunday visits—Scotch pancakes came top in our estimation; next, those hard little iced biscuits with pictures on them (she must have saved them from Nairobi visits), and finally her famous and delicious eggless, sugarless, flourless cake (it was made from bananas). She was our 'adopted' aunt, and we were her adopted family—this relationship lasted until she went to heaven. We adored Auntie Lorna.

My Sundays were crowded with good memories, of interesting things and lovely people. Of course it was comparatively easy for us in rural Africa; the sun shone, and the dehumanizing pace and pressure of western urban living were far away. There was no television and we hardly ever saw a paper. There was an advantage in possessing a venerable wind-up gramophone, with 78 rpm records—we could take it on Sunday picnics!

Granted our varying environments and cultures, is it possible to plan the first day of the week around certain 'different' facets? The meals? I now think of Sunday as a bacon and egg day—it's an enhancement after a week of cereal only for breakfast. And people to share the meals with? Within the family of a local church it ought to be possible for the 'adoption' scheme to take off—single people adopting a family; a family adopting a student, a widow, an overseas visitor. This takes thinking out and planning.

Who shall we bring to church? That shut-in person? That neighbour who is nervous of religious people? That fellow-student? Sunday is an opportunity for us Christians to broaden our horizons in acts of kindness, hospitality, witness and service. Without doubt many of these actions will revolve around the worship and youth activities of a local church.

But it needs a plan. Otherwise Sunday can simply degenerate into a day of aimless inactivity; or conversely we may find ourselves sucked into a vortex of

exhausting church activities and become chronic
sufferers from 'meetingitis'! Think it through. Pray it
through earlier in the week. Who is the preacher? I
will support him with my prayers! The musicians and
singers, the wardens and stewards, the Sunday School
and the youth... let me take nothing for granted. And
what about money? The apostle Paul approved of
planned giving:

> On the first day of every week, each of you is to put
> something aside and store it up, as he may prosper...(1
> Cor 16:2 RSV).

Christian giving is infinitely more satisfying and
exciting when thought and care go into it—as is true
with any gift. Let us not be satisfied with giving that is
on the *tipping level*. We shall find that the greater the
hold the good news has upon our lives, the greater will
be our desire to contribute financially to the church's
work and outreach. Nobody is going to twist your arm!
Ultimately it is *hearts* that God wants, not cheques.
But if an individual has learnt to give regularly, sacri-
ficially and strategically to the mission of the church, it
is an unmistakably sure sign of spiritual growth!

Care, planning and prayerful forethought need to
go into our use of the Christian Sunday. And, finally?

Protect it

Why? Simply because nobody else will protect Sunday,
apart from ourselves. If the commercial people were to
get their way, the ringing of the church bell would very
soon be replaced completely by the tinkling of the cash
registers, the clicking of the turnstiles, and the rumble

of traffic taking thousands of men and women off to another day of work.

The best way to protect Sunday is to use it properly, always remembering that Sunday is a *day*! It is not an hour of casual worship, somehow fitted into the diary. We learn to block the day out as special, as the highlight of the week.

Of course, worship is the focal point. We are going to be in communication with the Creator! We are going to praise the name of his Son, Jesus Christ—which means much more than making a joyful noise or repeating endless Hallelujahs. If I were to say to my Australian dentist, 'Oh, Denise, I praise you; I truly, truly praise you,' she might give me a very strange look. But if I were to say to her, 'Denise, your care and skill in filling those cavities is remarkable—and you never cause me a twinge of pain!'—*that* is true praise. *To praise in worship is to make great affirmations about our God.*

And we shall learn together as we worship. Take notes on the sermon! It will keep the preacher on his toes apart from anything else. Jot down the headings and the Bible references on paper, and see if you can follow them up afterwards. The preaching may leave something to be desired—never mind; sit up and take notes anyway. I once heard a sermon on St. George and the Dragon. The biblical content was nil. But I took notes assiduously and so kept awake.

Praying for a needy world, reading from the very word of God, identifying with Christ's family—many elements go into Christian worship. It is not like sitting in a concert hall, where it is largely immaterial whom you may be sitting next to. Sunday is not a private day, it is a family day. It matters that the family should come together. Prize this opportunity that comes every week; plan it carefully, and protect it by never taking it for granted. Sunday is special. It's bacon and egg day! Or, if you prefer, avocado day.

* * * *

To learn: Revelation 1:17,18. Hold onto this verse of scripture; it will reassure you on countless occasions!

His body broken once for us
is glorious now above;
The cup of blessing we receive,
a sharing of his love:
As in his presence we partake,
His dying we proclaim
Until the hour of majesty
When Jesus comes again

—CHRISTOPHER PORTEOUS
(*Hymns for Today's Church*, Hodder & Stoughton)

8

Eating and Remembering

If you were to take a visitor from space and confront him with the great pyramids of Egypt, he could hardly fail to exclaim, 'What are they? What are they *for?*' Their towering structures dominate all else. The same is true of Nelson's Column, the George Washington obelisk or the Eiffel Tower.

Some of these great monuments are tombs, commemorating the mighty leaders of history. But for Jesus there is no tomb. The man who towers over all others, who divides history into BC and AD, left no memorial. He never even wrote a book. All he did was to take bread and wine on the eve of his death, and distribute it to his few friends. 'Eat this...drink this...in remembrance of me', he directed them.

The friends of Jesus have been doing this ever since. 'But why?' a stranger might ask. 'What does it mean?'

Centuries before Jesus came, the same question was being asked about the Israelite Passover feast. In the words of Moses:

And when your children say to you, 'What do you mean by this service?' you shall say, 'It is the sacrifice of the

97

Lord's Passover, for he passed over the houses of the people of Israel in Egypt, when he slew the Egyptians but spared our houses' (Ex 12:26,27 rsv).

Give yourself ten minutes to think about the bread and wine of the Jesus meal, and its remarkable link with the ancient feast of the Passover. For you and I—if we are Christians at all—will be sharing in this service of remembrance not once or twice, but on scores, even hundreds of occasions! Let's get a firm understanding of what the Holy Communion is all about. First of all, when was it instituted?

This is significant! The New Testament record informs us: 'Then came the day of Unleavened Bread, on which the passover lamb had to be sacrificed. So Jesus sent Peter and John, saying, "Go and prepare the passover for us, that we may eat it"' (Lk 22:7,8 rsv).

Ever since the people of Israel were delivered out of Egypt under the leadership of Moses, the Passover had been held to commemorate this great act of redemption. God's people were never to be allowed to forget it. Now on the threshold of a greater and universal redemptive act—the cross—it was Passover time. This was no coincidence; Jesus had clearly planned to institute his Supper as a new Passover. That Thursday night was a *transition* night between the old and the future order. It is a pity that many Christians take part in the Holy Communion without ever having been informed about the background of the Passover.

What, broadly speaking, happened in the Passover? After prayer, the head of the house passed round a cup of wine with the words: *Blessed be thou, O Lord our God, King of the world, who hast created the fruit of the Vine.* Next there passed from one to the other a kind of salad of bitter herbs. These reminded the participants of their former suffering under the Egyptians. The herbs were eaten after being dipped in a sauce made up of almonds, nuts, figs and other fruits—the sauce itself, being red in colour, reminding all present of the hard labour of brickmaking imposed by their former taskmasters.

Then a second cup was passed round, and the meaning of the Passover was explained by the household leader. Two unleavened loaves or cakes were then taken; one of them was broken, and the pieces placed one on the other. With a prayer of thanks one of the pieces would then be dipped in the sauce and eaten, along with part of the sacrificial lamb and the herbs. Everyone would follow suit.

A third cup followed—'the cup of blessing', which was accompanied by a prayer of thanks from the leader. Then a fourth cup was distributed, and after that a hymn would be sung (see Psalms 113–118). Sometimes even a fifth cup would be added, together with further singing from Psalms 120–127. Have you followed up to now?

On the night of Jesus' betrayal, what probably happened was that Jesus would have been *transforming* the Passover as he went along.

And he took bread, and when he had given thanks he broke it and gave it to them, saying, 'This is my body which is given for you. Do this in remembrance of me.' And likewise the cup after supper, saying, 'This cup which is poured out for you is the new covenant in my blood' (Lk 22:19,20 RSV).

The result was a new service, built on the old, but with a new concept at its heart—the sacrificial death of the Lamb of God. Here was a new deliverance, a new covenant, a new order, and the apostle Paul was aware of this as he wrote to his Christian friends: 'For our Passover Festival is ready, now that Christ, our Passover lamb, has been sacrificed' (1 Cor 5:7 GNB).

The Holy Communion takes different forms, according to culture and tradition—but basically what we do in this service goes right back to that upper room where Jesus met with his friends. And where is the emphasis to be placed? What are we supposed to be thinking? Let's look at it in five different ways.

The backward look—we commemorate

'Do this in remembrance of me.' But why? The reason is plain—we forget too easily. Supposing there were no observance of this Lord's Supper? Over the years we might feel inclined to merge the death of Jesus with all the other great New Testament events; to say in effect, 'Of course it was important, but so were the baptism of Christ, the healings, the teaching, the great example he set us.' Indeed some of us run away from *blood*—it hardly seems right to focus on something so ugly in our sophisticated era.

The Holy Communion pulls us up repeatedly; the cross is important, the cross is absolutely central in the life of a Christian. Eat, drink and remember what it cost for you to be forgiven! We look *back* to that one great sacrifice for sin. It can never be repeated. Although in our service we are dramatizing what Christ has done for us, in no sense are we *repeating* the sacrifice, or offering Christ afresh. If you want confirmation of this you will find that Hebrews 9:25–28 is conclusive on this point. Take time to read it.

For it is a table that we come to in the Holy Communion, not an altar! An altar is for sacrifices, but the unique sacrifice for sins has already been made. Let us then follow the example of the Anglican Book of Common Prayer (and its modern counterpart), in which any mention of the Communion Table as an 'altar' is studiously avoided. The Lord's Supper helps us to look back to what Christ has done, once and for all . . . and we are grateful.

The upward look—we communicate

It is not a dead Christ that we worship and commune with when we meet in this way. Traditionally it is an empty cross, not a crucifix, that is the symbol of the Christian faith. Our Master is alive—and as we receive the symbols of bread and wine, we are irresistibly reminded of his love and of his presence, and are drawn closer to him.

It is not that there is intrinsic power in the bread and wine as such. The Communion is a sacrament of the gospel; it is a 'visual aid', dramatizing the historical fact of the body and blood of Jesus given for us in a violent death. The bread and wine are the outward symbols of an inward and spiritual reality—namely, feeding upon the Lord by faith in our hearts. No superstition should be attached to these visible symbols. They remain, simply, bread and wine, and they are not to be the objects of our worship. And yet . . . and yet . . . they *are* powerful symbols! Just as a photograph will remind us vividly of a loved one, and even seem to bring them closer, so it is with the symbolism of the Lord's Supper. The theologians call this *dynamic symbolism*—the Holy Communion is no *mere* memorial. In taking the bread and wine we are communicating with the risen Christ, and he with us. Result: we are reassured of his presence, we are reshaped—and re-vitalized!

The inward look—we appropriate

The body of Christ...the blood of Christ...Eat this ...drink this. Yes, we understand well that these are figurative terms. The bread *represents* Christ's body to us. But for some there is a problem. 'It sounds too horrible,' they say. 'It sounds almost cannibalistic. What am I supposed to be thinking as I eat and drink?'

The Bible's use of imagery can help us here. The psalmist of old spoke of his enemies who 'came upon me to eat up my flesh' (Ps 27:2 RSV). What did he mean? He meant that these evildoers intended to take advantage of him! A similar phrase occurs in the account of the three mighty men who risked their lives to obtain water from the well of Bethlehem. They brought it to King David, but he was so moved at their bravery that he was unable to drink the water. Instead he poured it out upon the ground as an offering to God:

> Far be it from me, O Lord, that I should do this. Shall I drink the blood of the men who went at the risk of their lives? (2 Sam 23:17 RSV).

Such a phrase could only mean that David felt unable to take advantage of the possible deaths of his three henchmen.

Apply this, if you will, to the action of eating and drinking in the Holy Communion. As we symbolically partake of the body and blood of Christ, in actual fact *we are taking advantage of all that his death achieved on our behalf.* We are once again reminded of the love of God, of his full and free acceptance of us, of what it means to be justified, forgiven, liberated, of our membership of the family of God and the life of heaven.

In that moment of closeness to our Lord, we appropriate afresh the blessings he has won for us by his death.

The outward look—we participate

'Take this', said Jesus, 'and divide it among yourselves' (Lk 22:17 RSV). This was not, first and foremost, a private and individualistic affair. It was a family gathering, a sharing. The apostle Paul called it 'a participation' in the body and blood of Christ (1 Cor 10:16 RSV). He reminded his readers that, just as the many pieces of broken bread all came from the one loaf, so we all, though many people, are one body in Christ. We belong to each other!

Grudges, then, are not to be harboured among Christians who share in this family occasion. We are one body. Stockbrokers and panel beaters, teenagers and octogenarians, church leaders and novices—as forgiven sinners we are on the same level at the foot of the cross. And we are to love one another in this sharing fellowship.

The forward look—we anticipate

The Lord's Supper has a time limit fixed upon it. We shall not be holding these services in heaven! For then our communion with Jesus Christ will be direct, face to face. In the meantime his fellowship, his presence and his love are mediated to us in a number of ways, and what better way than through the remembrance meal he commanded us to observe? But not for ever!

> For as often as you eat this bread and drink the cup, you proclaim the Lord's death until he comes (1 Cor 11:26 RSV).

One day...he'll be back. So, in a strange way, the Supper, which seems on first evidence to be pointing backwards, is also a sign-post to the future. To Christ's return. To glory. To the Supper which will end all suppers!

People and events are remembered in different ways. We have birthday cakes; we have tombstones, we tie knots in our handkerchiefs. *Learn to value the Holy Communion.* It brings Calvary—and Christ—very near. Think of it! Who were Napoleon, Garibaldi and Charlemagne? They lived centuries nearer to our time than did Christ; and yet Napoleon, Garibaldi and Charlemagne are dust-laden with antiquity—while Christ is near enough for us to talk to him, and derive strength and comfort from his living presence.

*   *   *   *

To learn: 1 Peter 3:18.

Group Work: Pray for God's illumination, and then read Isaiah 53:1–12. Ask yourselves these questions as you study this wonderful passage:

1. Although the prophet lived centuries before the time of Jesus, what is it about this passage that points us so clearly to Christ? Let each study member choose a sentence or phrase.

2. What phrases in this passage remind us of the Old Testament Jewish sacrifices?

3. Look at verse 4. Can you think of various New Testament episodes that illustrate this sentence both in the life and in the sufferings of Jesus? In what way could it be said that he was smitten by God? Compare your answer with Matthew 27:46.

4. Why did Jesus Christ die? Which verse more than any other explains the reason? How would you explain this to a modern person?

5. What does this passage teach the follower of Jesus about reacting to adversity or persecution?

6. Is there a single sentence in this passage in which the truth of justification is foreshadowed? Can you remember what justification is?

7. Can we, biblically, justify the use of this passage in speaking of Christ? *Clue*: Try Acts 8.

PART THREE

The Freedom Fighters

To Satan, the more thou hurtest and goest about to hurt me, the more proud and stout I am against thee, and laugh thee to scorn. The more thou terrifiest me, and seekest to bring me to desperation, so much the more confidence and boldness I take, and glory in the midst of thy furies and malice; not by my own power, but by the power of my Lord and Saviour Christ, whose strength is made perfect in my weakness.

Martin Luther, from his commentary
on the Letter to the Galatians

Failures, you see, are only temporary tests to prepare us for permanent triumphs

—CHARLES R. SWINDOLL

9
The Fight

Tennis was always my great love. But until I beat Miller my rating was little more than zero at my secondary school. I met Miller in the last eight of our under-sixteen tennis tournament. The runaway favourite for the event, Miller, was quite an impressive-looking player. He was confidently expected to cruise past me to the semi-final.

It was shameful, the way I beat him. I had my plans laid. I deliberately arranged to play him on a day when there was plenty happening at the school. The tennis courts were unoccupied; nobody was present to witness our encounter. Miller roared away with the first set—he was all over me. I looked like heading for a rapid exit from the tournament, clean and quick.

That was before I started my lobbing tactics! It wasn't nice, but it worked. The awesome drives began to lose pace. The smashes were going just out of court. Running like a rabbit I managed to level the score. And by the end of the final set *I was all over Miller!* I never lost to him again, and within a short while I was in the school team. Psychologically the match did something to me. It earned me the reputation of 'the fellow who had beaten Miller'—a reputation I had to live up to. From that day my game improved by leaps and bounds; I was beginning to realize that I could win!

We can hardly believe the possibility of winning, when we first start out as Christians. We had come to take sinful habits and attitudes for granted. We were one-dimensional people, geared to this life alone, trapped by materialism, living for ourselves. Indeed we were so helpless that we had no idea of our predicament.

Then one day the picture changed. The Liberator came! He sliced through those bonds that held us captive, and threw them into the grate. He scooped up the heavy weights of guilt that had anchored us to the floor, and tossed them out of the window. He picked up a heavy iron poker lying in the corner, and said: 'See that intruder at the door? Take this, and go and deal with him.'

But we hesitate. 'Great Liberator, can't you go? You're so much stronger!'

'No,' comes the reply. 'I've already dealt with him a long time ago; he knows he's beaten. Now it's your turn. *You can win.*'

An amazing thing happens as we take up our weapons. We discover that when we resist wrongdoing and evil, as we deliberately *choose* for Christ and his standards, the opposition gives way. We find to our astonishment that we are able to beat down Satan under our feet!

But who is Satan? He is evidently part of the created angelic order. The angels were not created as evil beings, for everything in God's creation was good (Gen 3:1). But there is enough in the Bible to indicate that part of the angelic world, headed by Satan, chose to rebel against the divine authority, and fell (2 Pet 2:4; Jude 6). Satan, then, is the originator of sin and evil. But he is not all powerful, and he is certainly not on a level with God. The Bible never teaches what is called 'Dualism'—God and the Devil are not co-equal. Satan is not divine, has no independent existence, is not all-knowing and has a limited existence. His destruction is already assured (Rev 12:12; 20:10).

But he is powerful enough! Through a spell-binding variety of stratagems and deceptions, his power exerts itself on all five continents. We must not be surprised at the discovery that, in making friends with God, we have also made a great enemy.

Fortify yourself with the breathtaking realization that good is stronger than evil; that our adversary met his match at Gethsemane and in the victory of Easter; that what we see today are not the pulsating vibrations of a kingdom in ascendancy. They are the thrashing death-throes of a kingdom in desperation!

> ...the prince of this world is coming. He has no hold on me... (Jn 14:30 NIV).

> In this world you will have trouble. But take heart! I have overcome the world (Jn 16:33 NIV).

> And having disarmed the powers and authorities, he made a public spectacle of them, triumphing over them by the cross (Col 2:15 NIV).

> Since the children have flesh and blood, he too shared in their humanity so that by his death he might destroy him who holds the power of death—that is, the devil—and free those who all their lives were held in slavery by their fear of death (Heb 2:14,15 NIV).

> You, dear children, are from God and have overcome
> them, because the one who is in you is greater than the
> one who is in the world (1 Jn 4:4 NIV).

> ... the devil has gone down to you! He is filled with fury,
> because he knows that his time is short (Rev 12:12 NIV).

Open the New Testament where you will; the same
wonderful theme is woven into it—Christ is the great
Winner, while death, darkness and despair are the
great losers. It is Christ's victory, first and foremost.
As we identify with him and choose his way for our
lives, so his victory becomes our victory. We have
changed over to the winning side. It is to the cross, and
Easter, that we can look back with confidence.

'Now that you've changed sides,' I once said to a
new Christian, 'you're like the newly naturalized
Frenchman who was asked how he felt on becoming
English. He replied, "Ah, *mon ami*, that is simple.
Waterloo used to be a great defeat. Now it's a victory!"'

But let us be practical. What do you do when you
are tempted? Those old habits and attitudes, that
explosive temper, the gossip and scandal-mongering,
the cutting of corners, the relentless pressure on our
sexual standards, the vanities, excesses and secret
vices? *What do you do when you are tempted?* Think about it
a moment. Don't leave the question for the preacher to
sort out. This affects the plumber and the politician,
the scientist and the student; it raises issues that must
be worked out in boardroom and bedroom alike.

Trouble think

Some of us don't even fight, when it comes to resisting
the pull of unbelieving society. We quietly succumb,

and then lie down, dismally signalling for the ambu-
lance to arrive! Failure seems built into our thinking.
We have visited exciting meetings where everything is
'Praise the Lord!' and 'Hallelujah!' This can deepen
the sense of depression: We find ourselves thinking
along these lines: *Am I alone in my struggles? Have all these
marvellously successful people left me at the starting gate?
What a dreadful person I am! Who can get me out of this state?*

Worry not. The great apostle Paul echoed these
sentiments—as an advanced believer!

> What a wretched man I am! Who will rescue me from
> this body of death? (Rom 7:24 NIV).

If Paul felt the strain of engaging in a battle for
holiness and control, it is hardly surprising that others
should feel the same. Yes, it *is* a fight; we were promised
nothing less when we started out on the Christian
road. What makes everything worthwhile is that
Christianity is true, and that we have entered into a
state of friendship with God! Besides that, nothing else
matters; the fight, the inconvenience, the failures even.
We *are* accepted, just as we are, failure rate and all.
There will be occasions when, for the umpteenth time,
we fail and hear that insidious whisper 'Call yourself a
Christian? You're a fine one to ask for forgiveness—
you said that only yesterday . . . and the day before.'

Don't give up! We are sinners, and shall remain
sinners for the rest of our lives, but *accepted* sinners,
nonetheless. Let us not focus our gaze upon those
Christians who seem to be so amazingly triumphant
and successful (for sinners they remain too), but rather
upon Christ. He is our goal—and he is also our friend
and our encourager. Let us see if we can learn from the

times of failure, and ask oursleves, *Why did I falter? What had I forgotten? How can I do better next time?* There is always a next time! Begin to think positively. Think of the possibilities. Think about winning. Remember Miller...

Double think

We are devious creatures. All too easily we can rationalize our failures, and find convenient scape-goats. One of them, of course, is the devil. You may have caught yourself murmuring: 'Well, the devil was too strong for me this time.' *Implication:* 'It's not really my fault—the devil is so powerful!' This is the road of resignation. Alternatively there is the road of extremism. We will meet with well-meaning believers who immediately assume that an evil spirit is the cause of someone's difficulties. We are told that the evil spirit of temper, of lust, of hatred, must be *prayed* out of the sinner. I have met many who have suffered from this mistaken form of counselling. Six weeks after their 'deliverance' they are more confused than ever.

Naturally we clergy do indeed meet with people who have become entangled with the world of spirits (usually through deliberate involvement with occult practices); but this is very, very different from the daily struggles we are all involved in, against ingrained habits and attitudes! And the power of the devil against a Christian? It is limited to that of *temptation*. We cannot be forced to do wrong. If we as Christians sin, it is because we *choose* to sin. The responsibility is ours, not the devil's.

'Double think' has, at times in Christian history, taken the form of *perfectionism*. This is an exaggerated

view of sanctification. Its devotees claim that at some
point or other, usually after some crisis experience
subsequent to conversion, they have become totally
delivered from all sin; they have arrived! Frankly I
have very rarely encountered this error in such an
extreme form, but we must not be surprised if it pops
up in some form from time to time. It leads people
down the blind alley of pride, sometimes of gross
immorality, resulting always in confusion and
severance from reality. A good dose of grammar is the
answer! Read on.

'...And so we have these three "tenses" of salvation,'
concluded the speaker at a students' conference I
recall attending. 'I *have been* saved, initially, from the
penalty of sin by a *crucified* Saviour.'

The sound of ballpoint pens scribbling frantically
on paper was almost deafening as the points of the talk
were elaborately made and noted down. I was hearing
them for the first time.

'Next,' continued the erudite gentleman, 'I *am being*
saved, progressively, from the *power* of sin by a *living*
Saviour. This goes on all my life.'

I banged the information into my notebook, and
looked up expectantly for the next point.

'And thirdly,' I heard, 'I *shall be* saved, finally, from
the *presence* of sin altogether by a *coming Saviour*. This
occurs when I die, or when Christ returns to earth—
whichever happens first.'

I put down my pen with a sense of achievement. In
three deft sentences the speaker had given me the
doctrines of justification, sanctification and glorifi-
cation—the perfect answer to perfectionist double
think!

Bubble think

Back to our question again: What do you *do* when you are tempted? We have all known the experience of doing precisely nothing. We have caved in without a struggle, conforming quietly and unprotestingly to the standards of society. 'After all', we murmur to ourselves, 'God will forgive; it's all right. I'm a Christian. Hallelujah anyway!'

Something's gone wrong? You failed? Um…well …it's probably all right; praise the Lord…

Bubble think; we've most of us been guilty of it. Standards *do* matter. We are in the service of a Leader who has jacked up the level of Christian behaviour to the very top. Being a disciple of Jesus is not a balloon ride; it is a fight. We are followers of the purest, the holiest being of our entire human story. This will involve us in moral, and perhaps costly, decisions every day.

'So what did you do when they turned the lights out?' I asked my brother. He had been telling us of a party he had been invited to. The drink had been flowing freely. Then the lights went out.

'It was impossible to leave,' he explained. 'I just tried to take evasive action. There was a Christian girl there in a similar predicament. We finally solved it by both getting on top of the table in the darkness, and talking to each other earnestly about our respective study courses!'

Character is what you are in the dark. So said the nineteenth-century preacher, D. L. Moody. How right! It is a wonderful liberation to have our sins forgiven, to be free of the nagging ache of secret sins and vices, to live a life that is open for all to read—even if we are aware of doing battle on virtually every front!

Must it be battle? Yes, we shall never be free of it. Perhaps we thought, on entry into the Christian family, that we were going to be set free from conflict and inconvenience. For most of us, however, our struggles *began* at that point! Were we promised anything less? Christ came and gave us the gift of his Spirit, not to set us free *from* the fight, but to set us free *for* the fight.

So what do you do when you are tempted? In plain terms, *you choose not to sin*. It is as simple, and as inconvenient, as that. It is inconvenient, because, to be perfectly frank, it is much easier to go along the old familiar path of self-pleasing. And Christ's way? It is, of course, strange and novel—and often very inconvenient. But it is not impossible. He has put his Spirit within us; the power is available.

So making progress in the battle is not a hopeless quest for power to win through. The power is there, it truly is! The issue again and again concerns the *motivation*—do we *want* to win? If an individual has the desire to win, then it is entirely possible to say to the tempting adversary, 'Sorry Satan, not today!'

'And how can I improve my motivation?' a new believer once said to me. The answer is very simple: *Enlarge your vision of Jesus Christ*. Meet his people. Read from his word. Communicate with him in prayer. Feed upon him by faith at his Table. Little by little the reassurance will penetrate our thinking: *You can win*. Sure, we will make mistakes. There may be times when our unseen opponent seems to be all over us. But the encouraging New Testament picture is that in all these things we can be 'more than conquerors through him who loved us' (Rom 8:3 NIV). Remember Miller ... We are going to beat down Satan under our feet!

* * * *

To learn: 1 Corinthians 10:13. It's a longish one; but try repeating it in the face of severe temptation, and you may find that by the time you have got to the end of the verse, you've forgotten what the temptation was!

And it's—Oh, the Briary Bush
That pricks my heart so sore;
And if once I get out of the Briary Bush,
I'll never go in any more!

—FROM AN ENGLISH FOLK SONG

10

The Briary Bush

'The Battle of Hastings reached its crisis right here,' I said, as I pulled the car in to the side of the little winding road that links the Sussex towns of Battle and Bexhill-on-Sea. Together my passenger and I gazed over the hedgerow at the site of one of the world's famous battles. It was on this undulating patch of green, dotted with trees, that the invading Normans had 'stuck' in 1066, unable to dislodge Harold's forces from their strategic ridge—until a ruse finally enticed the English down the hillside to their own defeat. The field in front of us had been the point of crisis.

Although I am no student of war, I have observed that in many military campaigns there comes a certain 'sticking point', a crisis, when little or no progress is made. The battle rages around this critical spot until a breakthrough of some sort occurs. Wasn't it a little farmhouse at Quatre-Bras upon which the Battle of Waterloo finally turned? Or the bridge at Arnhem? Or Boca House at Goose Green?

We who are Christians come to learn that our own progress often hinges, similarly, upon some critical issue. These sticking points vary considerably; fear of others, conceit, sexual impurity, false teaching or prayerlessness. A believer can be pinned down and reduced to ineffectiveness, potential unrealized and little more than a passenger in God's kingdom. Any one of a number of strategies can bring this about.

None of us is impregnable. We all have our Achilles' heel—that is true—but the astonishing upturn of Christian experience is that a man or woman can be overthrown not at their weakest point, but at their strongest! Look at Noah, noted for his outstanding righteousness. Only shortly after the epic of the flood, we read of him flat out on the ground, naked and drunk! Or take Abraham, hailed throughout the Bible as the man who believed God. At a critical moment we read of him, so doubting the divine assurance that Sarah his wife will give birth, that he takes another woman! Think of Moses who was 'very meek', yet tempestuously acting in presumptuous disobedience and so forfeiting a glimpse of the promised land. Or David the shepherd and psalmist, renowned for his soaring love—but guilty of both adultery and murder in a mad loss of control. And what of Peter, the intrepid fisherman, the courageous Rock Man, reduced to stammering invective in the face of a girl's chance question? These examples, and many more, should cut us down to size!

> Therefore let any one who thinks that he stands take heed lest he fall (1 Cor 10:12 RSV).

Many years ago a demolition firm evidently took as its advertising slogan the words 'We could wreck the pyramids'. Perhaps they could ... but could they *build* the pyramids? Far easier to pull down than to build up! A beautiful canvas can take even years to paint; all can be destroyed in thirty seconds' vandalism with a sharp knife. And how often we have seen this happen in character! In the public arena and in the private, it happens to politicians, showbusiness people, bankers, builders and sportsmen. Nobody is inviolate. The moment of toppling is usually preceded by a steady erosion of defences over a long period. It is the way of the opposition—to work us slowly into a position where our effectiveness is nullified, where our potential has evaporated into thin air. Most Christians know the experience of being pinned down in no-man's-land, of becoming 'stuck'. Or, to change the metaphor, we have become entangled in a briary bush. Somehow we have strayed from the recognized path of Christian discipleship and we are up to our waist in trouble. 'If once I get out of the briary bush', we resolve, 'I'll never go in any more!'

Can we learn from the Bible and from Christian experience, and be alerted to some of the tactics that will be used against us? Here is perhaps the most common of all.

Immobilized by defeatism

It can happen! Defeatism is a highly contagious malady. Theologians of a certain 'God-is-dead' brand have been peddling their wares for some decades now. I remember meeting one of these individuals. 'Why are you studying theology?' I asked him. 'It amuses me,' was his reply.

These are the people who love to talk about 'The Post-Christian Era'. Of course their message has no power to galvanize anything or anybody—only to immobilize! You can hardly imagine writing a hymn for this strange new religion. But steadily this gospel of negativism drips its way insidiously into colleges, religious television programmes and schoolbooks. After a while these ideas pick up some credence and you find yourself thinking: *Perhaps there is something in this; maybe 'God' is nothing more nor less than myself; perhaps I'm in the last generation of Christians there's ever going to be?*

We begin to wonder whether the Bible has power to change people any more. Is there any point in organizing outreach campaigns? Why bother about church, about prayer, about fellowship? We are becoming immobilized!

How do we counter this theology? We counter it by... *theology!* The true brand, the genuine article. The stupendous, life-changing truth that God in Christ has identified with this poor struggling world, born in a stable by the virgin Mary; coming among us in love and in supernatural signs; dying upon a human gallows to lift the guilt of sin off our backs; rising again from death to be its everlasting conqueror; ascending to the place of power and sending us the energizing gift of the Holy Spirit; guiding us, inspiring us, sending us as his representatives into all the world until he returns at the end in person to collect us! *Theology*.

You can always recognize its adherents by their optimism and activity. I think of my uncle, Keith De Berry, who even after retirement tirelessly preached, travelled and encouraged. I remember him, when he was in charge of a church, actually organizing conferences for people *who were going to become disciples*. Naturally these individuals were blissfully unaware that they were going to become followers of Jesus Christ, still less that there was a conference being carefully arranged for them!

We don't have to be beaten down by the defeatist attitudes that prevail in the west. We are not living in the post-Christian era in any case. It is more exciting than that. *We are living in the pre-Christian era.* It is a kind of Greek world that we are in at present, with umpteen beliefs, heresies and odd-ball outlooks rubbing shoulders with each other, much as they did when Paul the apostle came to Athens. Thousands around us have no idea who Jesus Christ is. This represents not a call for retreat, but for mobilization! But let's look at another of the tactics that we are bound to face.

Compromised by secularism

We are probably in the most materialistic society that the world has ever known. Films, books, television consistently imply that the sky is closed off, that God is but a concept, that standards of behaviour and morals are all relative and fluctuating; that there is no norm. It is not altogether surprising that some of these lies rub off onto Christians. But not all are taken in.

'But surely, when it comes to sex outside of marriage, there must be *some* exceptions?' It was a TV programme. David Frost was interviewing Billy Graham. I waited for the American's answer.

'No, there are no exceptions. None at all.'

'But certain mitigating circumstances, you'll surely concede? Is sex outside of marriage *always* wrong?'

'Always wrong. In every case. God's standard is fixed.' Billy Graham's granite faith was not to be shaken. I looked next day for the newspaper's comment on the interview: *Billy Graham mopped the floor with David Frost.*

Is it surprising that the man of the Bible came out on top? At least we have a firm standard given there. Without that we are in the realm of instant rules, chaotic families and blind morality. Secularism adjusts the rules as it goes along. There can be only one end to that, reminiscent of a situation that developed in a Lancashire town.

'I notice,' said the owner of the clock shop, as the factory watchman walked by, 'I notice that every day you set your watch by my clock here.'

'That's right,' said the watchman. 'I sound the buzzer at the factory, and I like to have it accurate.'

'But didn't you know?' replied the shop owner. 'There am I every day setting my clock by your buzzer!'

If we take our standards from each other, the trend can only be downwards. It is as we focus once more on the Ten Commandments, the Sermon on the Mount, and above all on the supreme example and standard set by Jesus Christ, that we can recall our generation from compromise and drift to a better way of living; to the lifestyle of the kingdom.

But on to another aspect of the briary bush.

Mesmerized by extremism

If you read through the New Testament letters, you will see that the major problem threatening the infant churches was that of false teaching. In letter after letter the inexperienced Christians had to be warned against teachers who purported to offer a richer or 'fuller' faith. This was the 'Christ-plus brigade'. In the letter to the Galatians, the issue was Christ-plus-circumcision. At Colosse the apostles faced a Christ-plus-super-spirituality involving angel-worship, visions and an authoritarian observance of various regulations. Faith in Jesus Christ *alone* is not acceptable to the false teacher. And how plausible he can sound to the new convert!

Can we construct a sort of identikit of the false teachers? Briefly, we can recognize them as follows:

(i) **They are the truth-warpers**. Error, plain and simple, we could recognize. But this is the half-truth, floated on apparently impeccable Bible orthodoxy! The extremist will take a healthy biblical topic like baptism, and blow it up into a divisive *issue* (Paul faced the problem in 1 Corinthians 1:10–17). Imperceptibly the biblical message of justification by faith alone is changed into justification by baptism, or—as in the case of the Galatians—circumcision. We have to beware of the new ritualists who would love to sweep the unwary into their own authoritarian systems.

(ii) **They are the sheep-stealers.** The extremists have, for the most part, very little spiritual power. They are not good evangelists and seldom make converts of their own from stone-cold unbelief. Where they excel is in *proselytism*—in hovering on the edges of churches and student fellowships where there is life, and using these as a convenient pond to fish in. Wherever you find a living fellowship, you can be sure that the sheep-stealers are in close attendance!

(iii) **They are the side-trackers.** First they dazzle. Then they distort. Finally they divert. They will fasten onto the side-issues and focus our gaze on these. The 'curiosities' of Scripture are made to become centralities! Before long we have left the mainstream of Christian living and are becalmed in a side-water.

(iv) **They are the peace-breakers.** The sects and the

extremists do not see themselves as *part* of a great fellowship. They are *It*! They cannot be content with other groups, with the various church denominations. Consequently, if they gain a toe-hold in a Christian fellowship, they will not be inclined to follow the leadership so much as to undermine and infiltrate it.

As we advance in our knowledge of the Bible, we learn to sift out the truth from error. We follow the example of the seventeenth-century Puritan, Richard Baxter, who declared, 'We should so lay the foundation of truth that error will fall by itself.' And so it proves to be. There is little point in naming the various extremist groups; their time is limited. After all, what do you know of Nestorianism, Apollinarianism, Eutychianism, Arianism or Sabellianism? These deviations all plagued the Christian church in the early centuries. History indicates, however, that the 'Isms' all turn to 'Wasms' eventually, while the church plods gamely on!

Let's look at one last aspect of the problems presented by the briary bush. Immobilized...compromised...mesmerized...and finally...

Neutralized by pietism

Our opposition will have done well if Christian energies can be safely *contained* within the boundaries of a singing, praising huddle of worshippers. It's nice being with a company of like-minded friends, as I have discovered. Those are often the moments that I wish could be perpetuated, when you feel at peace and at ease, surrounded by warmth and love.

But we cannot stay like this. To remain securely cocooned in a kind of compartmentalized 'Christian' existence is to run away from our responsibilities.

There is an unattractive form of judgmentalism that writes off the world as beyond all hope—and then smugly retreats into its own safe bunker. We must never write off any situation or any person, simply because to do so is completely out of character for a follower of Jesus.

The temptation is a very subtle one. You can feel so *spiritual*, meeting with your fellowship group, joining in worship and generally soaking up the good things of Christian living. But to do so, and to ignore the great Christian imperatives of shaping and changing the structures of our society is to get entangled in a briary bush with a religious shape to it! We have become innocuous, harmless, ineffective. No Christian community is likely to make much of a dent upon this world if its activity is limited to a bunch of Christians singing choruses to each other. Naturally, we need all the fellowship we can get. But this must then serve as a springboard for the penetration of our culture, neighbourhood and place of work. In the end you can divide people into two groups. There are those who live on this planet as sponges, absorbing and receiving all that they can. There are also those who are here to serve and to contribute. Which category do you fit into just now?

The briary bush may take many different forms. Happily there *is* a way out of it, if we have become entangled. But let's not make the experiment—our troubles will be enough without that complication! I like the words of evangelist Luis Palau: *He doesn't expect us to be perfect, but he does expect us to learn control. He doesn't expect sinlessness, but he does expect maturity. And he does not expect us to do this alone. He is the One who has begun the work in us, and he has promised that he will finish it.*

*   *   *   *

To learn: Try the second part of 1 John 4:4.

Group work: After prayer, read Ephesians 6:10–20. The apostle Paul is encouraging his friends in the Christian fight, with this portrayal of a Roman soldier. The following questions may help you to study this passage:

1. There are a number of direct commands scattered through this passage. Try and identify them. Taken together, what sort of impression do they convey of Christian living?

2. Look at verses 11 and 12. What is the nature of the conflict we are engaged in? When were you first aware of adversity and opposition in your own life as a Christian?

3. 'The whole armour of God' (v.13). Go through these pieces of armour slowly. Try and work out together what each piece stands for. In practical terms, how do we put the armour of God on?

4. What attitude of mind should be the Christian soldier's? Various indications are given in the passage.

5. What positive encouragements can we derive from Christian warfare? What sobering lessons need to be learnt?

6. What do you do when you are tempted? Share experiences!

People often think they have not strength enough; the fact is we have too much strength

—D. L. MOODY

I I

The Pathway to Power

I shall never forget the man whose talk one evening tipped me into Christian discipleship. I never got particularly close to him. He was not striking to look at; his athletic prowess was nil; he was neither clever, exciting nor witty. But for sheer effectiveness as a Christian, I can hardly think of anyone who could match him. How could such an apparent nonentity be so powerful? The people who found God through his work and witness ran into hundreds upon hundreds.

This makes you and me feel wistful. No, perhaps we are not going to be among those who win hundreds of others to Jesus Christ—but we do want to be *effective* for him in this world. How can we be more like Christ? How can we tap the very energy of God and be used in his service? How is a man or woman filled with the Spirit?

It is the question that has tantalized and teased generation after generation of Christian believers. There must be some talisman, we think; some additional secret of power into which we must be initiated, before we can really take off. But amazingly this is not true! The secret of spiritual power is not shrouded in impenetrable mist. The reason why we stumble and falter in our quest is that the people who experience the filling and fulfilling power of God are not self-conscious people at all. They never direct the spotlight onto themselves; they are not saying, 'Have you been filled with the Spirit? I have!' Always, always they are directing attention away from themselves.

They are praying people, but they never brag about their prayers. They are witnessing people, but you do not hear about their spiritual conquests. They are noted, not for their glib talk or spiritual clichés, but for their dependability, lack of sham and interest in *others*!

There, in part, lies our stumbling block. We have become used to the world of showbusiness and to the cry 'Look at me!' Perhaps this has to be—'spectacle' is the essence of entertainment. But true Christian living and spiritual power are not spectacular at all:

> For consider your call, brethren; not many of you were wise according to worldly standards, not many were powerful, not many were of noble birth; but God chose what is foolish in the world to shame the wise, God chose what is weak in the world to shame the strong...(1 Cor 1:26,27).

This has always been God's way. A stable, a few shepherds, the artisan home of a carpenter, a bunch from the Israeli fishing industry shortlisted as apostles, the ignominy of a criminal's death, the anonymity of a borrowed grave.

Has it sunk in? There is nothing flamboyant about the transforming power of God, mighty though it is. 'We have this treasure in earthen vessels,' wrote Paul, 'to show that the transcendent power belongs to God and not to us' (2 Cor 4:7 RSV). Think of the world's most famous jewel, the Kohinoor Diamond. It would be unthinkable to display it for public view in a jam jar! But this is the enigma of Christianity. That Japanese businessman lunching at his office desk in Tokyo, that window cleaner on the balcony in Frankfurt, that girl serving you at the MacDonalds outside Madison Square Garden... *earthen vessels*. The praying widow in a lonely apartment may be one; the harassed student revising for those finals could be another—men and women who have been surprised at what is possible through the energizing, in-filling power of God the Holy Spirit. Strangely, they find themselves able to take on new tasks, to face unwelcome adversity in a way that, earlier, they would not have dreamed possible.

But what is this pathway to power? I'm afraid we may have to reverse and un-learn earlier ideas, because Christianity tends to stand the world's concept of power on its head. The power of God in our lives! How can we experience this?

When dying is rising

Here is the first up-turn of our values. The world bids us preserve our life. Pamper it. Hedge it around with protection, insurance and every kind of buffer. Build it up and make it strong. Jesus taught differently:

> If any man would come after me, let him deny himself and take up his cross and follow me. For whoever would save his life will lose it, and whoever loses his life for my sake will find it (Mt 16:24,25 RSV).

Denying oneself is not 'self-denial'. It's not giving up

Coke, or doing without chocolate! It is to recognize that on the day we turned to Christ, the obituary notice appeared. Part One of our lives was flushed away into the past. It was dead and finished. We no longer stood under the condemnation of sin. The old set of factors and principles that governed our life no longer held true.

I can remember the day when Britain's currency went decimal. The old system no longer applied—it was dead. And, of course, we all had to start thinking decimal, because there was no point at all in going back to the earlier phase. Not that it is impossible to think back in terms of pounds, shillings and pence; indeed, every now and then I catch myself doing it even today. But it is completely unnecessary and illogical to do so—and it certainly doesn't help.

So it is, with the old and the new in spiritual terms. My old life is a distant phase now. It's dead. I'm sorry to say that at times I slip back into the old ways of thinking and acting; but it's quite illogical to do so. The obituary notice was written a long time ago: *We know that our old self was crucified with him [Christ] so that the sinful body might be destroyed, and we might no longer be enslaved to sin* (Rom 6:6 RSV).

Perhaps on the day that we 'died' to self-interest, self-ambition and self-centredness, we felt that we had lost something of ourselves. Then, as the days passed, we began to realize that we were properly 'living' for the first time! We had been, in New Testament terms, 'raised with Christ'. Things were different, better, newer. We were alive. To realize this is an epoch-making step forward in the pathway to spiritual vitality. We may consider it as having already happened (Rom 6:11). Volume One is over. Volume Two has begun! A second secret:

When slavery is freedom

Of course this is related to the first. 'The religion of
Jesus is a religion of resurrection', wrote Toyohiko
Kagawa of Japan. But it is also a religion of *liberation*.
We could hardly believe it, to begin with. We were
under no illusions, of course; to surrender to Christ is
no mere trip. This was reality—we were handing over
the keys of our lives to him. We may have felt hesitant.
Up to now, we thought, *we* had had the control of our
lives and destinies. Now we were surrendering them.
It was somewhat alarming.

Have we yet understood that this was not quite the
true picture? Have we grasped the sober fact that in
phase one of our biography we were far from possessing
control of our lives? We were under another authority
altogether, and could do nothing about it! The New
Testament tells us that we were *slaves of sin*. We were
victims of a situation that would eventually destroy us
altogether. When we turn to the greater power of Jesus
Christ, we move from living under one authority to
another.

William Penn said in 1681, 'If we are not governed
by God, then we will be ruled by tyrants.' That is
perfectly correct. We cannot live without authority in
our lives. The difference between the two main rival
authorities, however, is staggering. One is destructive,
the other is life-giving. One crushes individual identity,
the other enhances it. One overrides the personality,
gradually robbing it of creative expression; the other
fulfils it, integrating and liberating it with the power of
love and with the energy of God's Spirit. Christians

are those who, 'having been set free from sin, have
become slaves of righteousness' (Rom 6:18 RSV). But,
as we have probably begun to realize, this is slavery
with a difference. It is not without reason that an old
prayer uses the phrase, 'whom to serve is perfect
freedom'! Let us move on:

When weakness is strength

We need continual re-education in this matter of
power. John Stott, speaking in a consultation on evan-
gelism in Thailand, declared emphatically:

> Now you and I may be very weak. I sometimes wish we
> were weaker. Faced with the forces of evil we're often
> tempted to put on a show of Christian strength, and
> engage in a little evangelical sabre-rattling! But it is in
> our weakness that the strength of Jesus is made perfect.
> It is words of human *weakness* that the Spirit endorses
> with his power. It is when we are *weak* that we are truly
> strong, because we put our trust in him.

Think about it...how true! When did Christianity
touch rock bottom in its attempts to win the world?
When was it *least* effective? History gives us ample
examples. Why, when it was trying to be powerful.
The Crusades of the Middle Ages! When we wave the
flag, flex our muscles and sing triumphalist hymns on
a victory march, the performance is all too likely to
turn into a Death March.

Apply this to opposition, adversity and suffering, if
you will. The world sees suffering as a dead end;
Christianity sees it as a gateway to progress and power.
Not that we *seek* persecution or affliction. Nor should
we feel guilty if at any one point we are not facing the

lions in the arena. But we should at least prepare to be on the receiving end of the anger that Christ's mission has generated. And when it comes, we can learn to treat it as part and parcel of Christian living.

'When suffering comes,' wrote Hugh Silvester, 'the Christian (if he is anything like me) says, "Why me? Why should this happen? Am I not a child of God?" He regards suffering as an interruption, an unwelcome interlude. When it is over he can get on once more with living a "fruitful" Christian life. Not so; suffering *is* the Christian life. "Since therefore Christ suffered in the flesh, arm yourselves with the same thought" ... (1 Pet 4:1)' (*Arguing with God*, IVP 1971, p.117).

The apostle John, suffering exile on the lonely island of Patmos, greeted his readers of the Revelation with the phrase, 'I John, your brother, who share with you in Jesus the tribulation and the kingdom ...' (Rev 1:9 RSV). *That's it!* The two go together in Christian living; poverty and power, grief and glory. We have seen it in Poland, we have seen it in Uganda, we have seen it in Korea.

You may not be suffering in any obvious way as a Christian just now. But learn from history and from the lesson that Paul and Barnabas taught their fellow-Christians of old, 'saying that through many tribulations we must enter the kingdom of God' (Acts 14:22 RSV). Deep down, we recognize the truth of this principle. Most of us have met Christians who have suffered. Have we not been aware of their strength of character, of a certain depth and power that they exhibit?

Paul the apostle faced affliction in many and various ways. At one point he referred to his 'thorn in the flesh'. He prayed that it might be removed. It was not.

'But,' we say, 'this was the mighty Paul! Could God not have given him recovery?' *It was not to be.* 'But he said to me, "My grace is sufficient for you, for my power is made perfect in weakness"' (2 Cor 12:9 RSV). This is the way of Christ; this is the way of the cross. At times we shall feel frail in our Christian calling; vulnerable, weak and hard-pressed. *Good*—it is better that, than the other. Ours is the way of power and victory. And finally?

When emptying is filling

We are commanded to 'be filled with the Spirit' (Eph 5:18). What does this mean? In this passage, the apostle Paul is contrasting two kinds of intoxication— that by alcohol and that by the Spirit of God. These two kinds of domination are poles apart! To be controlled by alcohol is to be *out of control*, impaired, helpless and useless. To be dominated by the Holy Spirit is to be integrated, fruitful and fulfilled. But how can we ensure that we are so filled?

The Holy Spirit is not an influence; he is a person. He can be grieved and lied to. But he is also *God*. The Scriptures tell us that he can be blasphemed against. He is the third Person of the divine Trinity. From the earliest chapters of the Bible we read of him being at work, in creation, in the inspiring of God's messengers, in his empowering of the church from Pentecost onwards.

His is the 'spotlight' ministry of glorifying the person of Jesus, of making him real in the life of a believer. The Holy Spirit does *in* me all that Christ did *for* me, applying the great benefits of salvation and making them personal. He gives power for Christian service. He gives abilities and gifts to every believer that can be used for the glory of God and for the building up of the church. Without him the Christian life grinds to a standstill.

I remember driving my car, when the haft shaft broke. Not that I knew this. All I knew was that my foot was flat on the accelerator, the engine was emitting a roar like a World War II Spitfire, but the car was stationary. *The power had gone.* This is what happens when, through neglect of the Bible, prayer and fellowship, we cease to depend upon the indwelling presence of the Holy Spirit. There may be plenty of effort, words and noise, but no actual movement or progress.

True, the Spirit indwells every real believer in Christ. We do not have to *wait* for him to come to us, as did those early disciples. Once we are past Pentecost in the Bible, *all* the tenses relating to the initiating work of the Spirit in the believer are in the *past*. We have *been* born anew by the Spirit (1 Pet 1:3); we have *been* sealed by the Spirit (Eph 1:13); we have *been* anointed (or commissioned) by the Spirit (2 Cor 1:21); we have *been* baptized in the Spirit and so made one with fellow-believers everywhere (1 Cor 12:13). The Spirit is the great Leveller; he is 'the democracy of Christianity', for by his initiating work we have all been made a living part of the international fellowship of Christ.

It is in the *continuing*, daily ministry of the Spirit that we must be obedient; we are not to grieve the Spirit; we must walk in him; we are to be filled—with a regular, repeatable filling. But *how* may I be filled with the Spirit, and so serve Christ more effectively?

It is very, very simple—but demanding nonetheless! *First, I must remove the blockages.* I must daily repent of those known sins which otherwise clog progress. That is obvious! The *Holy* Spirit is indwelling me; I can hardly be filled with his presence and power if I am deliberately holding onto my pet vices.

Second, I must submit to the rule of Christ in my life. As I take in from the Scriptures, I shall become aware of what Christ wants me to be like, of what he wants me to do. As I obey him, so the way is open for me to be filled for ever-increasing effectiveness.

Third, I must share my blessings with other people. The Spirit did not enter my life so that I could hug God's joy and blessings to myself. There must be an outlet! As, through prayer and service I give myself to others, I make a remarkable discovery—namely, that the way to be filled is to be emptied.

Have you not found this yourself? Somebody asks you to take on a piece of Christian service, hard, demanding, perhaps even frightening. At the end of the assignment, do you feel better or worse than you did before? *You feel better*! You feel filled, fulfilled—and deeply satisfied. This is related to the filling of the Holy Spirit.

In the best all-round teaching book on the Holy Spirit I have ever read, Billy Graham testifies: 'Personally I find it helpful to begin each day by silently committing that day into God's hands. I thank him that I belong to him, and I thank him that he knows what the day holds for me. I ask him to take my life that day and use it for his glory. I ask him to cleanse me from anything which would hinder his work in my life. And then I step out in faith, knowing that his Holy Spirit is filling me continually as I trust in him and obey his Word' (*The Holy Spirit*, Collins).

'Are you filled with the Holy Spirit?' When eager Christian friends have asked me that question, I decline to answer, because I notice from the New Testament that people filled with the Spirit never claimed this for themselves publicly. It was left to those who were acquainted with them to make the observation. So when you are ever asked about the Spirit's activity in your life, the scriptural reply, perhaps, should be, 'You'd better ask my wife... You'd better ask my boss!'

In the last analysis, the Spirit-filled person is more aware of Christ than he is of the Spirit, for it is the Spirit's work to throw the spotlight on Jesus (Jn 16:14). There is this strange anonymity about the Spirit. This is true in church life as well. What is the mark of a true 'Holy Spirit Church'? Without question it must be that Jesus Christ is seen to be at the very, very centre of everything that is going on!

Has it sunk in? The pathway to spiritual power is marked by a series of surprisingly paradoxical landmarks!

*   *   *   *

To learn: Can you try two verses? Romans 12:1,2.

We need constantly to remind ourselves that the Christian Way is worth following even if only a few are treading it, for it is the road leading to Eternal Life

—JANANI LUWUM OF UGANDA, MARTYR

12

Still on Track

'You have twenty-four hours in which to leave the country!'

Ken, a missionary friend of our family's, was given this ominous warning by the political authorities. An able joiner, he had been directing a Christian educational programme in Africa, only to get caught in the crossfire between rival ideologies. He had been on the verge of equipping a newly-built church with pews—there it was, standing empty. Now he was to be thrown out. Twenty-four hours to go!

How would you have spent those last hours? Rushing off to the bank to scrape your savings together? Charging around the neighbourhood like a whirling dervish, re-organizing everything in sight? Feverishly gathering all your precious belongings together? Desperately organizing an all-night prayer session?

Ken did none of that. His last twenty-four hours were spent in building *one* pew, very carefully, watched by his African pupils. Finally it was done.

'That's your prototype,' Ken told them. 'You make the rest of them like that! I have to go now.' With that, he left them with the solitary model on which to base their labours. He also left them, of course, with a superb model of how a goal-orientated Christian reacts to pressure.

It is, in the end, only the person with a sense of call who is still firing on all cylinders when the crisis moment strikes, who is still serenely on track twenty-five years after the start. It is the sense of call that keeps a believer undistracted by rival masters and by a thousand beckoning side-shows. Peter the fisherman was to re-learn this by the Lake of Galilee at a memorable breakfast party with the risen Jesus:

> Peter turned and saw following them the disciple whom Jesus loved, who had lain close to his breast at the supper and had said, 'Lord, who is it that is going to betray you?' When Peter saw him, he said to Jesus, 'Lord, what about this man?' Jesus said to him, 'If it is my will that he remain until I come, what is that to you? Follow me!' (Jn 21:20–22 RSV).

Follow me... The words found an echo in Peter's memory. It was by that same lake, three years earlier, that he had first heard the call of Jesus. An eternity had gone by since then. There had been the teeming crowds, the stirring miracles, the luminous parables. They had travelled the historic road to Jerusalem, witnessed the collision with religious authorities and shared in the memorable Last Supper. Then the nightmare of the arrest, the horror of the denial and its hideous sequel—desertion, trial and execution.

And now this! The Carpenter had had the last laugh after all. He was back from the cold, never to die again. Goodness had emerged from its tangle with evil as the undisputed master. 'Follow me!' came the command once again.

Who would *not* follow at such a juncture? You and I have been persuaded upon this very course some twenty centuries later. Never mind the ordeals that lie ahead. Legend has it that Peter the apostle was to be martyred. Ken the builder was to be expelled. Some people lose their jobs, their friends, their freedom because of their love of Jesus Christ. Somehow everything seems worthwhile because of him. It was certainly so with Peter by the lakeside that morning.

One part to play

A process of re-direction was still necessary. Peter had looked over his shoulder and seen the apostle John. Curiosity overcame him. 'Lord, what about this man?' he asked.

Jesus' reply has lessons for us all. *'What is that to you?'* was the rejoinder. *'Follow me!'* The temptation to be distracted by the destiny, the career, the gifts of others is almost irresistible at times. But we are to be ourselves. Christ has set us free from the burden of copying others, of wistfully longing after the roles fulfilled by our friends. You can spend a decade wishing your life away, if you are not careful. 'Only one life is allotted us,' wrote Alexander Solzhenitsyn, 'one small, short life!'

There will never be anybody quite like you again in the whole history of the world. There are to be no re-runs, no repeat performances! Let's not get hung up, then, on the success or achievements of others. Some Christians worry themselves to death on the gifts of the Spirit. It's not worth the hassle! We are not to be copybook replicas of each other. Of course, there are believers who want to make their fellows into cardboard cut-outs of themselves, to press *their* own gift and ability upon everybody else. One day they will learn better. Each individual has a precious identity and a potential that is unique. Nobody else is going to dictate how we live our lives. No powerful leader, no authoritarian group, no clergyman, minister or super-Christian is going to shape my affairs. Fellowship and advice I will always need, but in the last analysis I am a disciple of one Person only; I am responsible to precisely one call: *Follow me.*

Obedience to the call of Jesus introduces us to a whole world. We can't stay tied mentally to our own snug environment. As Christians we begin to learn what the Incarnation meant—to become identified with the needs and cares outside our own immediate boundary. Some of us will be required to bring our Christian insights into the field of money-making, politics, industry, pop music and art—*and to fulfil our own role in reclaiming these areas for God.*

We cannot do everything—but prayer focuses the life. Little by little, as we maintain contact with our unseen Director, we shall discover what we were put here to do, to be. We shall also learn the thrill of expanding our horizons and becoming part of a world network of prayer and fellowship. We shall learn how prayer traverses the oceans, ignores international boundaries, leaps over barbed wire. We shall begin to build up a list of people we pray for—in Bolivia...Sri Lanka...New Zealand. *Have you begun?* You could start today. One part to play; we must gradually establish what role God has carved out for us.

One place to look

'Follow ME', he said. That is it. There is one reference point to which we must turn constantly. It is our relationship to this Person that will protect us from going down a myriad of blind alleys, that will keep us intact when the world seems to be crumbling.

I have quoted from Solzhenitsyn. I quote him again, from his Templeton Award address given in London: 'Today's world has reached a stage which, if it had been described to preceding centuries, would have called forth the cry: "This is the Apocalypse!"'

It is an incredibly exciting era in which to live. Yes, it is a very dangerous one. We may see the destruction of civilization as we know it over the next years. Ours may be the task of re-building society all over again, from nothing. That is nothing new. It happened after the collapse of Rome centuries ago. We can be quite sure that if there is some kind of collapse in our civilization, partial or total, it will be the Christ-orientated people, and them only, who will have the sufficient spiritual energy to re-build.

You can tell the bystander from the front-liner very quickly indeed, just by attitude alone. Come to the Amalekite battle-front, back in the Old Testament, in Joshua's time. As reporters, we probe for information on the latest situation confronting the embattled Israelites.

'Well, it could be worse,' comes the reply. 'We've lost a quarter of our men in the last two hours, but we can hold on. Maybe you could ask them to send up a few more arrows and spears from the back—we're running a mite low here.'

And so to the back line. 'How are you getting on?'

'Oh, it's terrible, just awful. My tent leaks. And we had manna again for breakfast!'

That's the difference. Our conversation and attitude alone will reveal whether we are front-liners or simply uninvolved, grumbling spectators.

Take the fight seriously. Get a Christ-centred, biblical world-view for yourself. It will take a long time to formulate. Learn to read and interpret the Bible for yourself, and in the company of others. Not for us the vague, few 'proof-texts', valuable as verse-learning is. Let's learn to tackle the Bible in earnest, humbly submitting to its authority, and struggling with its great themes and concepts. As we turn its pages, we must ask ourselves: What is the *original* meaning of this passage; what did it mean to the first readers; what is the *natural* meaning? Let me not start playing games with words as so many deviationists have done. We also ask: What is the *general* meaning of what I am reading? How does it harmonize with the rest of Scripture?

Then there are books. If anything there are too many books! We have to learn discrimination in this matter—to try and pick out the books that are going to build us as people, always remembering that Good is the enemy of Best! Gradually, with care, discernment and discipline, a Christian learns to see the universe, the world as it really is; to see politics, law, sport, money, the family, sex, music and the media as Christ sees them.

Four hundred years ago a biblical world-view prevailed, in general, among thinking people in Europe. There was a general assumption of God above all and in all. That view has actually been eroded away today. To recover it for society is a Herculean task...but we have got to do it. It starts with Christ's call, as it came to Peter by the lakeside: *Follow me*. The one reference point! One place to look.

One plan to fulfil

What is the programme? FOLLOW ME. How do we see the agenda of world history? As the steady eroding of the world's energy resources and powers, to the point of extinction? As an evil take-over by authoritarianism and the powers of evil? As a cataclysmic military disaster, resulting in a lifeless nuclear desert? Christ taught differently.

We are heading towards a *conclusion*. It may indeed involve natural or military convulsions, but at the centre of everything will be a Figure upon whom every eye will be turned. We will not need to guess at his identity:

> Then I saw heaven opened, and behold, a white horse! He who sat upon it is called Faithful and True, and in righteousness he judges and makes war. His eyes are like a flame of fire, and on his head are many diadems; and he has a name inscribed which no one knows but himself. He is clad in a robe dipped in blood, and the name by which he is called is The Word of God....On his robe and on his thigh he has a name inscribed, King of kings and Lord of lords (Rev 19:11–16 RSV).

Christ will be back. He will be coming personally, publicly, visibly and with unprecedented power. His return will consummate the victory of Calvary. It will mark the eclipse of the old order and the downfall of the empire of evil that has plagued us all these centuries. All the iniquities and injustices of history will meet with their reward. The balances will be set right. The bodies of the faithful dead will be raised and glorified. Those who belong to Christ and are still alive will be caught up to meet with the returning King. Goodness will reign... permanently. It will be heaven!

'I want it *now*!' So bubbled an Asian Christian to me in our church entrance one Sunday morning. I had been preaching on the Last Things. I too wanted it all to happen. Happen it will, as surely as day follows night. Meanwhile you and I are here to usher in history's terminal point and goal.

If it is my will that he remain until I come, what is that to you? Follow me! So said our Lord to the enquiring and impatient apostle. Part of us is longing for the celestial sunrise, for the battle to be over. The other part of us recognizes the urgent needs of our struggling world. There is a calling to be fulfilled. It is not a question of looking for God to be relevant to our own lives, ambitions and plans. It is an issue about our own relevance to *him*, as the last chapters of human history unfold.

I remember one occasion when American evangelist Billy Graham visited our church. After several decades of non-stop preaching all over the world, there he was at sixty-five, proclaiming the good news with the same strident energy and buoyancy as he possessed at thirty. Men like him set us an example of costly dedication and sacrifice.

John Wesley was another. Never man *worked* like this man, was the judgement upon this remarkable evangelist of two centuries ago. In his lifetime he travelled the equivalent of ten times around the world on horseback in his determination to serve the interests of the kingdom. His last letter, written to William Wilberforce MP, was dated February 24th, 1791. In it he encouraged his Christian friend to continue the struggle for justice, recognizing that only a call from heaven could provide the energy for the job in hand:

> Unless God has raised you up for this very thing you will be worn out by the opposition of men and devils; but if God is with you who can be against you? O be not weary in well-doing. Go on, in the name of God and in the power of his might, till even American slavery, the vilest that ever saw the sun, shall vanish away before it.

Our little study is over. Perhaps you have never read a book on Christian beginnings before. Let us be prayerful that we shall always remain hungry for more, discerning the real from the counterfeit, obeying our call, remaining faithful to the Lord of the whole universe, until at the trumpet sound the heavens roll up, the elements dissolve and the supper party begins.

* * * *

To learn: Add John 14:27 to your list. Remember to review your verses, and let them become a basis for learning more of the Scriptures.

Group work: Pray together, and then read John 14:1–11. The following questions will stimulate discussion:

1. Try and understand the setting. Look back at the previous sentences. Look also at the opening sentences of chapter 18, after Christ's recorded words have concluded. How were the disciples feeling? How did Jesus' words match their feelings? Let members of the group pick out a word or a phrase of encouragement, in turn.

2. What does verse 2 speak to us about? Why is this terminology used by Jesus?

3. *A place.* How do you understand the future order? What corrections have taken place in your thinking since becoming a follower of Christ?

4. Look at Thomas' words, and Christ's reply to them, in verses 5 and 6. How would you use these words today, in today's religious and philosophical scene?

5. Supposing you meet with a devotee of a sect or group, who argues from verse 6 'Ah, yes, Jesus was THE way *for his time.* But since then there have been other revelations to supersede him.' How would you answer? Ponder and discuss this. Mark 13:21–23 may help.

6. Now for Phillip's question in verse 8. What was he wanting? How common is this desire? What is the great truth enshrined in verse 9?

7. How would you explain the way of becoming a Christian to another person? Can you think of verses that explain the two events, the two responses and the two promised gifts? Take your time over this. Work it out on your own. Rehearse a conversation with yourself!

How to Live the Christian Life

by Selwyn Hughes
author of *Every Day with Jesus*

Do you
wish the day was over before it has hardly begun?
get irritated by even the smallest problems?
find reading the Bible every day difficult and tiresome?
have trouble mastering temptation?
try to copy others instead of developing your own gifts?

We can cram our heads with doctrine, but that in itself will not keep us from the problems that rob our lives of the peace, joy and effectiveness that Jesus promised. This book points the way through such problems, helping us to become the kind of people God intended. It is a positive affirmation that we *can* get the best out of the Christian life.

Kingsway Publications